FPL
745.582

Best of *Bead&Button* magazine

Get Started

W9-AXK-739

Beading

DISCARD

DISCARD

Compiled by Julia Gerlach

FRAMINGHAM PUBLIC LIBRARY

SEP 1 4 2005

© 2005 Kalmbach Trade Press. All rights reserved. This book may not be reproduced in part or in whole without written permission of the publisher, except in the case of brief quotations used in reviews. Published by Kalmbach Trade Press, a division of Kalmbach Publishing Co., 21027 Crossroads Circle, Waukesha, WI 53186. These books are distributed to the book trade by Watson-Guptill.

Printed in the United States of America

05 06 07 08 09 10 11 12 13 14   10 9 8 7 6 5 4 3 2 1

Publisher's Cataloging-In-Publication Data
(Prepared by The Donohue Group, Inc.)

Get started beading / from the editors of Bead&Button magazine : compiled by Julia Gerlach.

   p. : ill. ; cm. -- (Best of Bead&button magazine)
  Includes index.
  ISBN: 0-87116-219-9

1. Beadwork--Handbooks, manuals, etc. 2. Jewelry making--Handbooks, manuals, etc. I. Gerlach, Julia R. II. Title: Bead&Button magazine.

TT860 .G48 2005
745.594/2

Managing art director: Lisa Bergman
Book layout: Kristine Brightman
Photographers: Bill Zuback and Jim Forbes
Project editors: Julia Gerlach, Pam O'Connor

Acknowledgements: Mindy Brooks, Terri Field, Lora Groszkiewicz, Kellie Jaeger, Carrie Jebe, Diane Jolie, Patti Keipe, Alice Korach, Tonya Limberg, Debbie Nishihara, Cheryl Phelan, Carole Ross, Candice St. Jacques, Maureen Schimmel, Lisa Schroeder, Terri Torbeck, Elizabeth Weber, Lesley Weiss

CONTENTS

INTRODUCTION

So many paths lead to beads. Some start with sorting through a beloved grandmother's costume jewelry. Some begin with an abiding interest in ethnic beadwork. Some commence with an innocent attempt to repair a favorite necklace. Whatever has brought you here, welcome! We're happy to have you with us in the exciting and colorful world of beads.

Beading is a wonderful creative outlet for the time-pressed and the stressed-out. It doesn't take much space or a large investment in supplies. It's also portable. In a small amount of time, often an hour or two, beading allows you to have a beautiful necklace, bracelet, or earrings to wear.

This book is a survey course on beading. You'll get a taste of all three main methods for creating jewelry with beads—stringing, wirework, and stitching or off-loom beadweaving. Give every one of them a try and settle into the one you like the best. But always remember that there is more room to explore.

Before you get started on a project, take a few moments to read the sections on "Tools and Materials" and beading "Basics." You'll find them frequently referred to in the directions to help you tie a knot or crimp a crimp bead or turn a loop. Nothing on these pages is hard to do, but some things will take a little practice to perfect. Once you are comfortable using the tools and techniques, there will be no holding you back.

And you couldn't have come to this art form at a better time. An abundance of bead supplies and suppliers—more than ever before—have made a dazzling array of materials readily available. For a start, you can find inspiring materials and terrific camaraderie at a local bead shop. You will also find wonderful online and mail-order merchants to entice you with beads and supplies from every corner of the globe. And if a bead show happens in your vicinity, don't miss it! You will be able to meet and purchase beads from glass beadmaking artists who create one-of-a-kind lampwork beads. You can also meet and buy from the worldwide travelers who collect and sell beads from Africa, Asia, and Europe.

It won't be long before you'll grow accustomed to creating the perfect necklace for a special occasion or making a unique and personal gift for someone you love. Then you'll wonder what you did before beads.

– *The editors of* Bead&Button *magazine*

TOOLS AND MATERIALS

It's easy to make beautiful bead jewelry that's as good as or better than the jewelry you see in upscale department stores. If you can thread a cord or wire through a hole, you're more than halfway there. The big "secret" of the pros is knowing what tools and materials to use to get the best results. On the following pages you'll find descriptions of the most important tools you'll need as well as commonly used findings and stringing materials.

FINDINGS

Findings are the parts that link beads into a piece of jewelry. Always buy the best metal findings you can afford. If you use base metal, it will soon discolor. Sterling silver and gold-filled findings usually increase the cost of a piece by less than $5 and look good for many years. Here are the key findings:

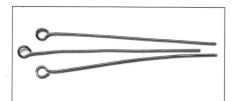

A **head pin** looks like a blunt, long, thick sewing pin. It has a flat or decorated head on one end to keep the beads from falling off. Head pins come in different diameters, or gauges, and lengths ranging from 1-3 in. (2.5-7.6cm).

Eye pins are just like head pins except that they have a round loop on one end, instead of a head. You can make your own eye pins from wire or head pins.

A **jump ring** is used to connect two loops. It is a small wire circle or oval that is either soldered or comes with a split that you can twist open and closed.

Split rings are used like jump rings, but they are much more secure. They look like tiny key rings and are made of springy wire.

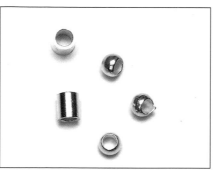

Crimp beads are small, large-holed, thin-walled metal beads designed to be flattened or crimped into a tight roll. Use them when stringing jewelry on flexible beading wire.

Bead tips are small metal container beads used to link a cord-strung necklace to a clasp while concealing the knots. (They are sometimes called calottes.) They come in either a basket shape or a two-sided, open bead shape. Basket bead tips hold the knot inside the cup. You squeeze the halves of bead-shaped bead tips together with the knot inside. The cord comes out the bottom of both.

Crimp ends are used to connect the ends of leather, suede, or other lacing materials to a clasp.

Clasps come in many sizes and shapes. Some of the most common are (from top to bottom) the toggle, consisting of a ring and a bar; the lobster claw, which opens when you push on a tiny lever; the magnetic, which consists of two halves that attract each other; the S-hook, which links two soldered rings or split rings; and the hook and eye.

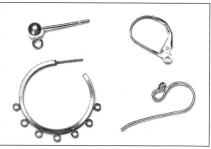

Earring wires come in a huge variety of metals and styles, including (clockwise from upper left-hand corner) post, lever-back, French hook, and hoop. You will almost always want a loop (or loops, as in the hoops above) on earring findings so you can attach beads.

Cones are usually made of metal and look like pointed ice cream cones with openings at both ends. They are ideal for concealing the ends and knots of a multistrand necklace and joining it attractively to the clasp.

Eyeglass findings come in two types. One is a small rubber band fastened in the middle to form two loops, the other is an elastic loop attached to a metal bead with a wire loop on one end.

STRINGING MATERIALS

Flexible beading wire comes in several brands. They all consist of very fine wires that have been twisted or braided together and covered with a smooth plastic coating. Aculon, Beadalon, and Soft Flex are the most popular brands and they all come in a variety of sizes. For many stringing projects, .014 and .015 work fine, but the weight of the finished piece is really what determines

what size beading wire you'll need. Use thicker varieties when using heavy beads or pieces that receive a lot of stress. Thinner wire can be used for lightweight pieces and beads with very small holes, like pearls. Some wires are more flexible than others. The higher the number of inner strands (between 7 and 49), the more flexible and kink-resistant the wire.

Bead cord is also commonly used for stringing beads. Made predominantly with braided synthetic fibers, some popular brands are Stringth and the thick upholstery thread Conso. They come in different thicknesses, which are indicated by numbers or letters; the higher the number or letter, the thicker the cord, except for 0, which is usually the thinnest. No matter how thick or thin, always use bead cord doubled when stringing.

Traditionally, pearls are strung on silk cord with a knot between each pearl, but many new nylon cords are almost as supple and much less stretchy than silk and knot beautifully.

Several different types of elastic cords are also made expressly for beading. Some elastic cords have a round profile and others are opaque and fibrous. Both types come in a variety of colors.

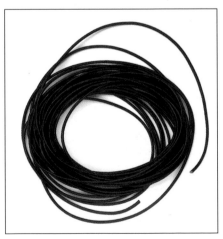

Leather or satin cord is usually used in designs in which the stringing material is featured rather than hidden.

Beading threads, primarily used for off-loom beadweaving, are often made with nylon; the most common is Nymo (the

small spools shown above, left). Nymo comes in sizes 0, B, and D, listed from thinnest to thickest size. Condition beading thread before use to prevent fraying, separating, and tangling. To condition unwaxed threads like Nymo, stretch it as you pull it through beeswax or Thread Heaven. Thread Heaven adds a static charge that causes the thread to repel itself, so it can't be used with doubled thread. To condition pre-waxed threads like Silamide, simply stretch it.

Recently, beaders have begun using fishing line in place of beading thread, specifically a brand called Fireline (above, right). Although it doesn't come in an assortment of colors, like Nymo does, its high-tech synthetic fibers make it a very resilient and strong thread. While it comes in various strengths, 6-lb. test Fireline is the one most often used for beading projects. Do not string beads on monofilament fishing line because it becomes brittle and snaps. Nor is sewing thread a good option for stringing or stitching beads as it is simply too weak.

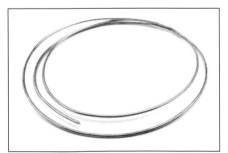

Wire is used to make loops and eye pins or to wrap beads creatively. The smaller the gauge, the thicker the wire. Memory wire is steel spring wire; it's used for coil bracelets, necklaces, and rings.

TOOLS AND MATERIALS

TOOLS

You need very few tools for making bead jewelry, but don't use the large, grooved pliers in your family tool kit; they produce terrible results.

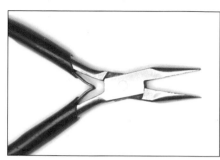

Chainnose pliers for jewelry making have smooth, flat inner jaws, and the tips taper to a point so you can get into tiny spaces. Use them for gripping and for opening and closing loops and rings. Some people call chainnose pliers flatnose because the inside of the jaw is flat. True flatnose pliers, however, do not come to a point at the tip, so they can't go everywhere that chainnose pliers can.

Roundnose pliers have smooth, tapered, conical jaws. You form loops around them. The closer to the tip, the smaller the loop.

On **diagonal wire cutters**, the outside (back) of the blades meets squarely, yielding a flat-cut surface. The inside of the blades makes a pointed cut. Always cut wire with the back of the blades against the section you want to use so that the end will be flat.

Do not use your jewelry-grade wire cutters on memory wire, which is extremely hard; use heavy-duty cutters or bend it back and forth until it breaks.

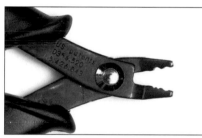

If you use crimps often in jewelry making, you'll want a pair of **crimping pliers**. Crimping pliers have two grooves in their jaws to enable you to fold or roll a crimp into a compact shape.

Split-ring pliers allow you to open split rings easily, without breaking your fingernails.

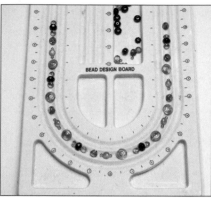

A bead design board is an important tool for visualizing your design before you start stringing.

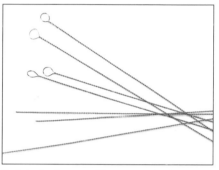

Twisted wire needles are made from a length of fine wire folded in half and twisted tightly together. They have a large, open eye at the fold, which is easy to thread. The eye flattens when you pull the needle through the first bead.

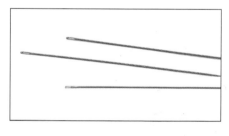

Beading needles look like extra thin sewing needles. The most frequently used sizes are #10 to 13. Higher numbers indicate a thinner needle.

BEADS, BEADS, BEADS

Beads are available in a dazzling array of shapes, sizes, and materials. From tiny seed beads to large gemstone nuggets, from natural wood and bone to sparkling crystal, from flowers to teardrops to cubes, spheres, and triangles, today's choices are nearly unlimited. Below is just a sampling of the bead types that can be had.

Czech seed beads

Japanese hex-cut cylinder beads

metal spacers and beads

briolettes

gemstone chips

Japanese seed beads

crystals (from left to right: bicone, cube, faceted round, and faceted drop or briolette)

gemstone nugget

Japanese cylinder beads

horn and bone beads

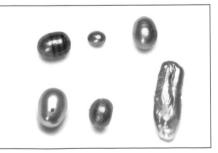
pearls (from left to right, top row: oval, rice, potato; bottom row: teardrop, button, stick)

pressed glass flowers and leaves

triangle beads

BASICS

To give your jewelry a professional touch and ensure that your treasures will stand up to frequent wearings, it's important to master a few techniques. Good knots, loops, and crimps can make all the difference between a piece you love and one that gathers dust in a drawer.

KNOTS

Working with beading cords and threads like Nymo, Silamide, or Fireline often requires knots for security.

half-hitch knot

Come out a bead and form a loop perpendicular to the thread between beads. Bring the needle under the thread away from the loop. Then go back over the thread and through the loop. Pull gently so the knot doesn't tighten prematurely.

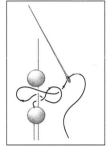

lark's head knot

Fold a cord in half and lay it behind a ring, loop, bar, etc. with the fold pointing down. Bring the ends through the ring from back to front then through the fold and tighten.

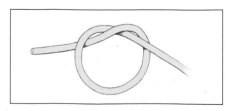

overhand knot

Make a loop and pass the working end through it. Pull the ends to tighten the knot.

square knot

1 Cross the left-hand cord over the right-hand cord, and then bring it under the right-hand cord from back to front. Pull it up in front so both ends are facing upwards.

2 Cross right over left, forming a loop, and go through the loop, again from back to front. Pull the ends to tighten the knot.

surgeon's knot

Cross the right end over the left and go through the loop. Go through again. Pull the ends to tighten. Cross the left end over the right and go through once. Pull the ends to tighten.

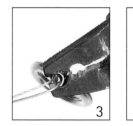

CRIMPING

Crimping, usually used to secure flexible beading wire to a clasp, is the process of flattening or folding a crimp bead securely on your stringing material. Flattened crimps require only a pair of chainnose pliers, while folded crimps require a pair of crimping pliers.

flattened crimp

1 Hold the crimp bead using the tip of your chainnose pliers. Squeeze the pliers firmly to flatten the crimp. Tug the clasp to make sure the crimp has a solid grip on the wire. If the wire slides,

remove the crimp bead and repeat the steps with a new crimp bead.

2 Test that the flattened crimp is secure.

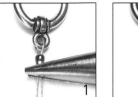

folded crimp

1 Position the crimp bead in the notch closest to the crimping pliers' handle.

2 Separate the wires and firmly squeeze the crimp.

3 Move the crimp into the notch at the pliers' tip and hold the crimp as shown. Squeeze the crimp bead, folding it in half at the indentation.

4 Test that the folded crimp is secure.

FOLDED CRIMP END

Folded crimp ends are used to connect leather or satin cord to a clasp.

1 Glue one end of the cord and place it in a crimp end. Use chainnose pliers to fold one side of the crimp end over the cord.

2 Repeat on the second side and squeeze gently.

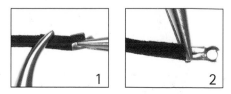

WIRE LOOPS

Wire loops are necessary any time you need to connect wire elements together, such as when attaching a beaded head pin to an earring wire. The basic plain loop is all that's necessary for many lightweight earrings, but for heavier items or anything needing extra security, wrapped loops are more appropriate.

If you've never worked with wire before, get some inexpensive craft or copper wire for your first attempts at making loops. Don't worry if your first loops aren't great; practice makes perfect. Your loops will be small if you form them closer to the tips of the pliers and larger if you hold the wire where the jaws are thicker. It's a good idea to mark your pliers with the exact place to grip the wire for a ³⁄₈-in. loop until you know it instinctively.

plain loop

1 Trim the wire ³⁄₈ in. (1cm) above the top bead. Make a right-angle bend close to the bead.
2 Grab the wire's tip with roundnose pliers. Roll the wire to form a half circle. Release the wire.

3 Reposition the pliers in the loop and continue rolling.
4 The finished loop should form a centered circle above the bead.

wrapped loop

1 Make sure you have at least 1¼ in. (3.2cm) of wire above the bead. With the tip of your chainnose pliers, grasp the wire directly above the bead.

Bend the wire (above the pliers) into a right angle.
2 Using roundnose pliers, position the jaws vertically in the bend.

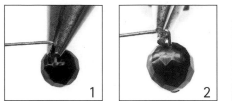

3 Bring the wire over the top jaw of the roundnose pliers.
4 Keep the jaws vertical and reposition the pliers' lower jaw snugly into the loop. Curve the wire downward around the bottom of the roundnose pliers. This is the first half of a wrapped loop.

5 Position the chainnose pliers' jaws across the loop.
6 Wrap the wire around the wire stem, covering the stem between the loop and the top bead. Trim the excess wire and press the cut end close to the wraps with chainnose pliers.

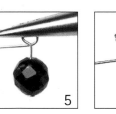

OPENING AND CLOSING LOOPS AND JUMP RINGS

Because wire gets brittle if it's worked too much, handle it as little as possible.
1 Hold the loop or jump ring with two pairs of chainnose pliers or chainnose and roundnose pliers, as shown.
2 To open the loop

or jump ring, bring the tips of one pair of pliers toward you and push the tips of the other pair away.
3 Reverse the steps to close the open loop or jump ring.

MAKING HEAD PINS

Make a tiny U-shaped loop at the end of the wire with the tip of a roundnose pliers, pinch it closed with chainnose pliers, and trim the wire end just above the bend.

WIRE BASICS

Wire comes in thicknesses called gauges. The higher the gauge, the thinner the wire, so 20-gauge wire is thinner than 18-gauge. If the wire is too soft, it may not hold its shape, but if it's too hard, it will tend to break. Wire sold as "half-hard" is a good bet.

Wire that's too hard can be softened by heating it with a torch. If your wire is too soft, you can harden it by hammering. Use a regular hammer with a smooth metal head if you also want to flatten the wire. If you want the wire to remain round, use a rawhide mallet. But beware: wire that has been hardened too much or twisted too many times breaks easily. It's best to harden it after bending. Don't hammer loops because you might create a rough edge. To avoid marking your wire, wrap the jaws of your pliers with cloth tape.

Always practice safety precautions when working with wire:
- Wear eye protection (safety glasses or the equivalent).
- When cutting wire, always hold both parts or cover it with your hand.
- File all exposed, cut ends smooth to prevent scratches or snags.

– *Carol H. Straus*

GALLERY

Crystal bib by Alice Korach

Peyote bangles by Mindy Brooks

Garnet necklace by Mindy Brooks

Fringed brick stitch necklace by Lisa Olson Tune

Raku and wire necklace by Wendy Witchner

Dichroic glass and crystal bracelet by Irina Miech

Ndebele herringbone bracelet by Cathy Collison

Focal bead necklace by Debbie Nishihara with art glass beads by Leah Fairbanks

STRINGING

Basic strung necklace

Requiring nothing more than the stringing of a colorful combination of beads and finishing with two crimps, this necklace is the perfect beginner beading project. Use a subtle blend of your favorite colors or mix them up as we did here. Once you've made this basic necklace, you'll want to make one to match every outfit in your wardrobe.

❶ Determine the desired finished length of your necklace (this one is 17½ in./45cm), add 6 in. (15cm), and cut a piece of flexible beading wire to that length.

❷ String a group of three lampwork beads separated by seed beads to the middle of the beading wire **(photo a)**. String a seed bead on each side.

❸ The seed beads act as spacers in this design, so make sure to string one between each of the main (lampwork) and accent (faceted quartz) beads. With a seed bead after each, string a faceted quartz, a group of two lampwork beads, a quartz, three lampwork, and a faceted quartz bead on both sides of the beads strung in step 2.

❹ After stringing the next seed bead, string a repeating pattern of two lampwork beads and a quartz bead three times **(photo b)** on each side. Test the length of your necklace at this point. If necessary, add another one or two quartz beads, again separated by seed beads, to make your necklace the correct length.

❺ When your necklace is the correct length, string a seed bead, a crimp, a seed bead, and half the clasp at one end. Go back through the last three beads strung **(photo c)** and crimp the crimp bead (see "Basics," p. 9).

❻ Pass the wire tail through a few more beads and trim.

❼ Repeat steps 5-6 on the other end of the necklace. Be sure to remove excess slack in the strand before crimping, but not so much that the necklace doesn't drape well.
– Gloria Harris

MATERIALS

- 16-in. (41cm) strand of 10 x 16mm lampwork or other glass beads
- 16-in. strand 9mm faceted blue quartz or other gemstone
- 1g size 8º seed beads
- 24 in. (61cm) flexible beading wire, .014–.019
- 2 crimp beads
- clasp

Tools: diagonal wire cutters, crimping pliers or chainnose pliers

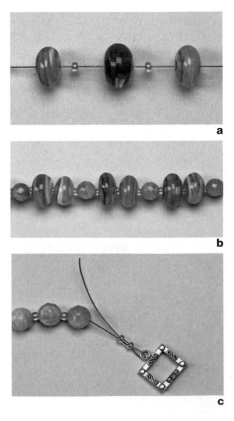

a

b

c

Two-strand bracelet

Beading doesn't get much easier than this. String together an assortment of pearls and crystals for a simply elegant double-strand bracelet that requires only a single crimp in its assembly. You don't have to attach a clasp, tie a knot, or wrap any wire loops to make this beautiful piece.

❶ Cut a 20-in. (51cm) strand of beading wire. Slide a 2mm spacer to the center of the wire and fold the wire in half. String the 12mm bead and four spacers over both wires (photo a).

❷ Slide one spacer onto each wire to separate the strands. String a pleasing mix of beads on each strand, placing a spacer after each one. String 6 in. (15cm) of beads for a 7-in. (18cm) bracelet. (Don't include the 12mm bead in your bracelet measurements.) As you work, consider how the strands look individually as well as when the two are next to each other. Try to place larger beads next to smaller ones and crystals next to pearls to create an interesting, balanced design. Make any adjustments in length before continuing to the next step.

❸ Slide a spacer onto each wire, and

a

b

c

then string a crimp bead over both wires (photo b). String spacers over both wires until you have enough for a loop that will fit over the 12mm bead. Take the wires through the crimp again and continue through a few beads on each strand (photo c). Tighten the beads by gently pulling on the wires until no wire shows between beads. Leave enough ease to keep the bracelet

MATERIALS

- 50–60 assorted 3-8mm pearls and crystals
- 75–100 2mm round sterling silver spacer beads
- 12mm bead for clasp
- 20 in. (51cm) flexible beading wire, .010 or .012
- sterling silver crimp bead

Tools: crimping or chainnose pliers, wire cutters

Optional: 10–15 assorted silver beads

flexible. Crimp the crimp bead (see "Basics," p. 9) and trim the excess wire.
– *Irina Miech*

Playing
with color

Take a long, hard look at your stash of beads. The bracelets and necklaces shown here require the brightest, boldest, and liveliest in your collection. Bring out your gemstones, crystals, metals, glass, and pearls in all manner of shapes, sizes, textures, and finishes. It's best to have your assortment laid out in front of you before you get started.

The next step is to try out various bead combinations. Now's the time to go beyond the familiar and comfortable color pairings you normally use. When you've found a new combination you like, set it aside and keep going. Let the beads surprise you.

When you're ready to start stringing, work in small sections and change color and texture every 1 to 2 in. (2.5–5cm). Incorporating silver or gold spacers among your beads will add definition to each color block and lend a sense of continuity to your finished piece.

These jewelry pieces are easy to string; the challenge is to design a pleasing and joyous array of colors. Experiment freely with your beads and be willing to do some rearranging before you crimp the final crimps.

MULTISTRAND BRACELET

❶ Determine the finished length of your bracelet, then subtract the clasp measurement to establish the length of the beaded strands. Add 3 in. (7.6cm) and cut six pieces of beading wire to that length.

❷ String a crimp bead on one strand, thread the strand through a loop on the clasp, and go through the crimp again (photo a). Tighten the strand so it encircles the clasp loop with some ease, leaving a 1-in. tail. Crimp the crimp bead (see "Basics," p. 9). Repeat five times, attaching two strands to each loop on the clasp.

❸ String a colorful mix of beads and spacers on each strand. The end beads must have holes large enough to accommodate two passes of beading wire, so you can hide the tails inside them (photo b). Check the way the beads look together and make any changes before you attach the strands to the other half of the clasp. Add or remove beads, if necessary, so the strands are the same length.

❹ Lay out the bracelet strands in parallel lines and place the second clasp half next to the unfinished ends. Make sure the clasp is correctly positioned so it will slide into the other half.

String a crimp bead on a beaded strand and go through the corresponding loop on the second clasp half. Go back through the crimp and a bead or two. Tighten the wire and check the strand for gaps between beads. Leave a little ease so the strand hangs freely, and then crimp the crimp bead (photo c). Repeat with the remaining strands. Trim any exposed wire tails.

SINGLE-STRAND NECKLACE OR BRACELET

Make an easy single-strand necklace or bracelet using the same basic stringing and finishing techniques.

❶ Cut a piece of beading wire about 3 in. longer than the desired length of your necklace or bracelet. String a crimp bead, go through the loop on one half of the clasp, and continue back through the crimp bead. Crimp the crimp bead.

❷ String multiple color blocks as shown in my pieces at left. When you've reached the desired length, string a crimp bead and go through second half of the clasp, the crimp, and a few beads. Tighten the loop and crimp the crimp bead. – Beth Stone

MATERIALS

multistrand bracelet
- assorted 2–6mm gemstones, crystals, metal beads, and seed beads
- assorted Bali silver spacers
- flexible beading wire, .013 or .014
- 12 crimp beads
- three-strand slide clasp

single-strand necklace or bracelet
- assorted 2–6mm gemstones, crystals, metal beads, and seed beads
- assorted Bali silver spacers
- flexible beading wire, .013 or .014
- 2 crimp beads
- toggle or lobster claw clasp

Tools: chainnose or crimping pliers, wire cutters

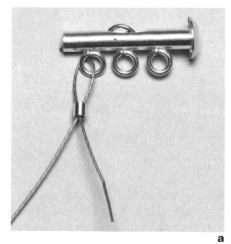

a

b

c

Easy Y-necklace

As much as fashion trends change, some designs always remain stylish. There have been many variations on the Y-necklace, and if you look through your jewelry box, you'll probably find at least one.

This Y-necklace has a versatile length of 17-18½ in. (43-47cm) with a 3-in. (7.6cm) dangle that ends with

a faceted labradorite drop. A converted six-hole clasp serves as the front connector component and the clasp. The next time you're in a bead store, stop and look at the different silver components available. You'll be amazed at how much fun it is to create a piece of jewelry around a silver charm or finding that catches your eye.

NECKLACE

❶ Cut a 13-in. (33cm) length of .012-.014 beading wire. String a crimp bead, pass the wire through a loop on the hookless clasp component, and go back through the crimp bead (photo a).

❷ Push the crimp up to the clasp and leave a 2-in. (5cm) tail. Crimp the crimp bead (see "Basics," p. 9 and photo b).

❸ String a garnet and a quartz bead over both wires and trim the tail (photo c).

❹ String a garnet, a labradorite, a garnet, and a quartz. Continue stringing this pattern (photo d) until the strand is about 7 ½ in. (19cm) long.

❺ String a silver spacer, a crimp bead, and a silver spacer. Pass the wire through the loop opposite the hook on the other clasp component. Go back through the silver beads and the crimp. Tighten the beads, leaving just enough ease for the necklace to hang nicely (photo e). Crimp the crimp bead and trim the tail.

❻ Skip a loop on the hookless clasp component, and using the next loop, repeat steps 1-4 (photo f).

❼ Repeat step 5 but pass the wire through the end link on the chain instead of a clasp part.

❽ String a labradorite and a garnet on a head pin. Make the first half of a wrapped loop (see "Basics") close to the garnet bead. Slide the loop through the end link of the chain (photo g), finish the wrap, and trim the wire.

❾ Cut an 8-in. (20cm) length of .010 beading wire. String the 28mm drop to the center of the wire. String a bead cap over both wire ends and down to the drop (photo h).

❿ String a garnet, a quartz, a garnet, a quartz, a garnet, and a crimp bead over both wire ends. Pass both through the bottom middle loop on the center component and back through the crimp bead. Pass them through a few more beads on the dangle, if possible (photo i). Crimp the crimp bead and trim the tails. If you can't get the wire ends through the gemstone beads, trim them close to the crimp bead.

BRACELET

❶ Cut an 11-in. (28cm) length of .012-.014 beading wire. String a crimp and a spacer on one end. Pass the wire through the clasp's loop and back through the spacer and the crimp bead. Crimp the crimp bead.

❷ String beads in the same pattern as step 4 of the necklace to the desired length, minus the length of the clasp.

❸ String a crimp bead and a spacer and attach the other half of the clasp as in step 1. – Cheryl Phelan

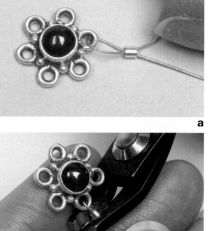

a

b

c

d

e

g

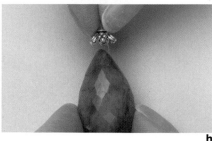

h

i

MATERIALS

necklace
- 28 4mm round garnet beads
- 11 15-18mm labradorite nuggets
- 14 8mm square dreamsicle quartz
- 28mm faceted labradorite drop, top drilled
- flexible beading wire, size .012-.014
- flexible beading wire, size .010
- 5 crimp beads
- bead cap, sterling silver
- 2-in. (5cm) head pin
- 4 3 or 4mm round sterling silver spacers
- 1½ in. (3.8cm) large-link chain
- decorative six-hole clasp

bracelet
- 11 4mm round garnet beads
- 5 15-18mm labradorite nuggets
- 5 8mm square dreamsicle quartz
- flexible beading wire, size .012-.014
- 2 crimp beads
- 2, 3 or 4mm round sterling silver spacers
- decorative clasp

Tools: crimping pliers, diagonal wire cutters, chainnose and roundnose pliers

Art bead ensemble

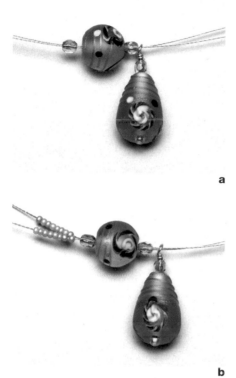

a

b

Lovely floral beads from India take center stage in this old-fashioned and feminine jewelry ensemble. They cost very little, but have a luxurious, Venetian-style appeal. Pair them with seed beads and fire-polished beads in complementary colors. If you can't find Venetian-style Indian lampwork beads, try other lampwork, glass, or even gemstone beads in these shapes.

The round beads are strung on two strands of flexible beading wire for support and body. The drop-shaped beads are perfect for dangles.

String one side of the necklace, gauging the design to reach half the desired length. String the necklace's other side to match and attach the clasp. Make matching earrings.

NECKLACE

1 Determine the desired length of your necklace. Subtract the length of the clasp from this measurement.

2 Add 6 in. (15cm) and cut two pieces of beading wire to this length.

3 String an 8º gold seed bead, a drop bead, and a fire-polished (FP) bead on a head pin. Make a loop or wrapped loop at the top of the pin (see "Basics," p. 9). Make two more dangles.

4 With the ends even, hold the wires together and string a dangle to the center of the wires. String an FP bead, a round bead, and another FP on both wires (photo a).

5 String eight 11º seed beads on each wire (photo b).

6 String an FP, a round bead, and an FP bead on both of the wires.

7 String a dangle, an FP, a round bead, and an FP on both wires.

8 Repeat steps 5-6 until you reach half the desired length determined in step 1. End with seed beads, adjusting the number at the end to reach the right length.

9 String the necklace's second side to match the first.

10 String a crimp, an FP, and a crimp onto both wires on one side. Bring the wires through the loop on the clasp and back through the first crimp. Try to fit both wires back through the FP and the next crimp. (I could only fit one of the wires back through the FP bead.) Tighten the wires around the loop. Crimp the crimp beads (see "Basics"). Trim the excess wire.

11 Adjust the beads along the necklace so there are no gaps. Repeat step 10 to attach the other half of the clasp.

MATERIALS

necklace
- 14–16 15mm Indian lampwork or other round beads
- 3 22 x 14mm Indian lampwork or other drop beads
- 20g size 11º seed beads
- 30–35 4mm fire-polished beads
- 55 in. (1.4m) .014 flexible beading wire
- 3 head pins
- 3 8º seed beads, gold
- decorative clasp
- 4 crimp beads

earrings
- 2 22 x 14mm Indian lampwork or other drop beads
- 2 head pins
- 4 bead caps
- 2 4mm fire-polished beads
- 2 French-wire earring findings

Tools: chainnose and roundnose pliers, crimping pliers, diagonal wire cutters

EARRINGS

1 String a bead cap, a drop bead, a bead cap, and an FP bead on a head pin. Make a loop or wrapped loop at the top of the head pin.

2 Open the loop of the earring finding (see "Basics") and slide on the dangle. Close the loop again. (Never pull out the curve of a loop because it stresses the wire and damages the loop's shape.)

3 Repeat steps 1-2 to make the second earring to match the first.
– *Pam O'Connor*

Beaded eyeglass holder

If you wear eyeglasses or know someone who does, here's an accessory that's both pretty and practical: a beaded eyeglass holder or "keeper." With the wide array of beads to choose from, you'll probably agree that a wardrobe of keepers is a necessity. (And if you get tired of wearing your keeper as a keeper, just put an S-hook between the two findings to turn it into a necklace.)

You can make your keeper like a single strand necklace but with an eyeglass holder finding on each end. If you have long hair, string some large beads near each of the findings to help the keeper hang straight down from your glasses, rather than tangling in your hair.

For a more casual look, you can use eye pins or wire to link together beaded units, as in the brown holder opposite.

Length can be variable, but for most people, 22-24 in. (56-61cm) long is about right. Symmetry is nice, as shown here, but you can also make some keepers as random as possible with never more than three identical beads together. It's fun to plan not to plan, but be sure to vary the size of the beads to avoid a boring, uniform look.

PEARL AND GEMSTONE HOLDER

❶ Plan and lay out your design before you begin stringing.

❷ Determine the finished length of the strand, add 6 in. (15cm), and cut a piece of flexible beading wire to that length.

❸ On one end, string a crimp bead and a seed bead. Go through the loop of one of the eyeglass holder findings and take the wire back through the beads just strung (photo a). Crimp the crimp bead (see "Basics," p. 9).

❹ String *a seed bead, a 6mm crystal, another seed bead, four pearls, a seed, a crystal, and a seed* (photo b). Add a gemstone, string from * to *, and string an accent bead (photo c).

❺ Repeat step 4 twice.

❻ String from * to * again and string an accent bead or a gemstone.

❼ To string the other side as a mirror image of the first side, string from * to *, add an accent bead, string from * to *, and string a gemstone.

a

b

c

d

e

f

❽ Repeat step 7 twice.

❾ String from * to * one more time, add a crimp bead, a seed bead, and the other eyeglass holder finding. Take the tail back through several beads. Tighten the strand so there is some ease but not too much, and crimp the crimp bead. Trim the excess wire.

MATERIALS

pearl and gemstone holder
- 16-in. (41cm) strand freshwater pearls
- 6 gemstones
- 6mm bicone crystals
- 8mm round crystals or accent beads
- size 11º seed beads
- flexible beading wire, .015
- 2 crimp beads
- 2 eyeglass holder findings

wire link holder
- assorted beads
- 5 ft. (1.5m) 20-gauge wire
- 2 eyeglass holder findings

Tools: chainnose and roundnose pliers, crimping pliers, wire cutters
Optional: S-hook

WIRE UNIT HOLDER

❶ Plan and lay out your design before you begin.

❷ To make a beaded wire unit, make a loop at the end of your wire (see "Basics"). Cut a piece of wire that will be long enough for the beads on the unit plus about ¾ in. (2cm). String the beads for that unit and make a loop at the other end (photo d).

❸ Make all your beaded units.

❹ To attach the units to form a chain, open one loop (see "Basics") on the first unit and string a loop of the next unit on it. Close the loop (photo e).

❺ Assemble all the units. When the chain is assembled, attach each end unit to an eyeglass holder finding (photo f). – *Karen Kinney Drellich*

Two-strand choker

String pearls and buttons to create a fresh looking choker that's done in a flash. The pearls offer a sophisticated look that can be dressed up or dressed down, depending on your button choice. Build the center of this choker first, then stop to check the button placement. Buttons should lie in the center third of the choker so they show on the front of your neck.

1 Hold the beading wire around your neck to determine the proper length for your choker. Add five inches (12.7cm) to that measurement, then cut it with wire cutters. Cut a second piece of wire the same length and set aside.

2 Make a button connector (photo a). Grasp one end of a ¾-in.-long (2cm) piece of 22-gauge wire with roundnose pliers. Curl the wire inward onto itself. Repeat on the other wire end. Make the loops small enough to fit through the button shank. Repeat to create five button connectors in total.

3 Thread one length of beading wire through a button connector. Pass the button connector through a button shank. Thread the second beading wire through the connector's other loop (photo b).

4 String 1¼ in. (3.2cm) of pearls on each wire. Push the pearls up to the connector (photo c).

5 Repeat steps 3-4 three times.

6 Repeat step 3, so five buttons are now strung and the necklace begins and ends with a button.

7 Tape the ends of the wire so the beads don't fall off. Hold the choker around your neck to check the length and button placement. Remove the tape and add or remove pearls between the buttons if necessary.

8 String pearls on one strand until they are 3 in. (7.6 cm) from the wire's end. Repeat on the other wire.

9 Tape the two adjacent wire ends together to prevent the pearls from slipping off.

10 Repeat step 8 at the other end of the necklace. Tape one wire end, leaving the other untaped.

11 String one silver bead, a crimp, and one silver bead on the untaped wire. Go through a loop on one of the clasp parts. Go back through the two beads

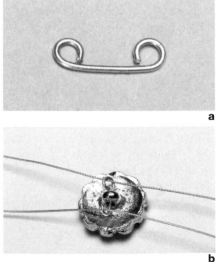

a

b

c

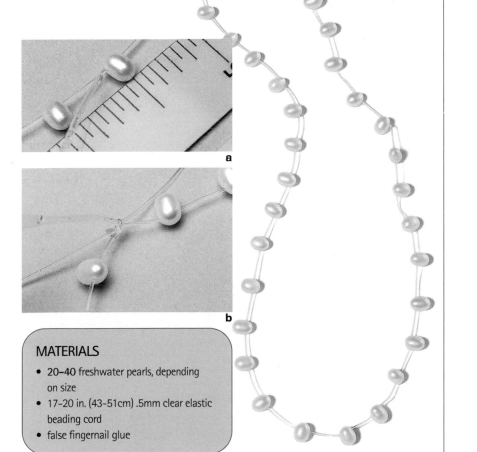

d

MATERIALS

- 5 buttons with shanks (figure buttons: Knot Just Beads, 414-771-8360)
- 60-160 pearls, quantity varies depending on pearl size
- 34-44 in. (83.8-111.7cm) flexible beading wire, .014 or .015
- 4-in. (10cm) 22-gauge wire
- 8 2-3mm silver beads
- 4 crimp beads
- toggle clasp

Tools: wire cutters, roundnose and crimping pliers, tape

and the crimp and tighten the wire to form a small loop around the clasp loop (photo d).

⑫ Repeat step 11 with the remaining wire on the first side. Snug up the beads and repeat at the other end.

⑬ Handle the necklace carefully so it doesn't come apart and double-check the length. Add or remove beads from each end as needed.

⑭ Crimp the crimp beads (see "Basics," p. 9) and trim the excess wire.

– Lynne Dixon-Speller

Floating pearls

Modern cultivation methods have made freshwater pearls available in a marvelous variety of shapes and colors at extremely affordable prices. So why limit yourself to stringing them into a demure strand of knotted silk? This fun and easy design uses clear elastic cord to give the illusion that the pearls are invisibly suspended around your neck.

❶ Cut a piece of elastic cord 3 in. (8cm) longer than the desired length of the necklace.

❷ String about half of the desired length with beads.

❸ Leaving 1¾ in. (4.4cm) at each end unbeaded, slide a bead near its place, put a dot of glue where it goes, and slide it onto the glue (photo a). Wait a minute before gluing the next bead.

❹ When all the beads are glued, tie the ends in a square knot (see "Basics," p. 9), leaving 1½ in. (4cm) tails (photo b). Glue the knot and trim the tails.

– Alice Korach

a

b

MATERIALS

- 20-40 freshwater pearls, depending on size
- 17-20 in. (43-51cm) .5mm clear elastic beading cord
- false fingernail glue

Beading with briolettes

Combine faceted stone or glass shapes with small silver tubes for a draping, two-strand necklace with an adjustable length. Don't stop here; add a few single-strand necklaces of different lengths to create a dramatic layered look.

STRING TWO CENTER STRANDS

❶ Measure your neckline and add 5 in. (13cm). Cut a length of flexible beading wire to this measurement.

❷ String a repeating pattern of one 4mm rondelle and one 6mm rondelle until the strand is about 6 in. (15cm) long. Carefully hold the strand up to your neckline. The beads should span between your collarbones. Add or remove beads as necessary.

❸ String three silver tube beads on each end of the strand and set aside.

❹ Cut a second length of beading wire 3 in. (7.6cm) longer than the first.

❺ String a repeating pattern of a 4mm rondelle, a briolette, a 4mm rondelle, and a silver tube bead until this strand is 1½ in. (3.8cm) longer than the rondelle strand.

❻ String three silver tube beads on each end of the strand.

❼ Lay the strands together so they are parallel and the rondelle strand is above the briolette strand. Pick up both wires at one end and string a 4mm rondelle over the wires and up against the silver tube beads (photo a). Repeat on the other side.

❽ Tape the ends to make sure the beads don't fall off the strands and carefully hold the strands up against your neckline to check the length. Look at how the strands lie together. If you would like the briolette strand to be longer or shorter, add or remove beads until you are happy with the length.

STRING NECKLACE SIDES

❶ String a pattern of seven silver tube beads and a 4mm rondelle over both wires on each side of the necklace until the necklace is the desired length. Each side should have the same number of beads and end with a 4mm rondelle.

❷ String a 2mm round silver bead, a crimp bead, and a 2mm round silver bead over both wires at one end of the necklace. Pass both wires through the end link on the chain and then back

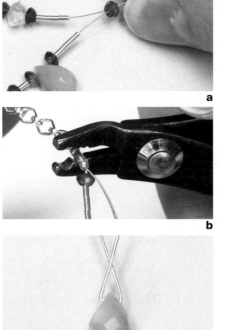

a

b

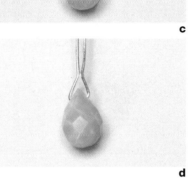

c

d

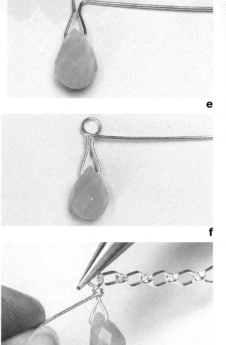

e

f

g

through the round silver bead, the crimp bead, and the second round silver bead.

❸ Push the beads up against the chain and crimp the crimp bead (see "Basics," p. 9 and photo b). Trim the tails close to the beads.

❹ Repeat step 2 at the other end of the necklace, but pass the wires through the loop on a lobster clasp instead of the chain.

❺ Pull the wires taut so there is no slack between the beads but make sure the wire isn't so tight that the beads bunch up. Crimp the crimp bead and trim the excess wire.

ADD A BRIOLETTE DANGLE

❶ String a briolette on the 22-gauge wire about 1 in. (2.5cm) from the end. With your fingers, bend both ends of the wire up until they cross above the center of the briolette (photo c).

❷ Use chainnose pliers to bend both wires where they cross, so they are

MATERIALS

- 18 7 x 10mm or 6mm briolettes, one to three colors
- 16 in. (41cm) strand 3-4mm faceted rondelles
- 26–30 6mm rondelles
- 10g 3 x 1mm silver tube beads
- flexible beading wire, size .012-.014
- 2 crimp beads
- 4 2mm round silver beads
- lobster claw clasp
- 3 in. (7.6cm) 22-gauge sterling silver wire
- 2 in. (5cm) large-link chain

Tools: chainnose and roundnose pliers, diagonal wire cutters

parallel to each other and side by side (photo d).

❸ Grasp the longer wire with chainnose pliers and bend it at a right angle about ⅛ in. (3mm) above the bend. Trim the short wire so it is flush with the right angle (photo e).

❹ Make the first half of a wrapped loop (see "Basics" and photo f).

❺ Slide the loop through the end link on the chain and complete the wrapped loop (see "Basics" and photo g). Trim the excess wire. – *Cheryl Phelan*

Beaded watch band

Utility is not the sole virtue of this watch. It's also attractive, unique, inexpensive, and easy to make. When you check the time, its beauty will ease that momentary panic when you realize, girl, you are LATE!

The project began when I found a watch on sale for a few dollars at a discount store. Its classic gold face with a celestial dial was fastened to a dull watch band and screamed out for a bead makeover.

I took my cue from the gold stars and deep blue of the celestial dial. Soon I had assembled faceted quartz beads, blue cathedral beads, and lapis lazuli beads with a few gold findings and was ready to make the transformation.

A variety of watch attachments and watch faces for beading are readily available in bead shops and from mail and online bead merchants. If you use a watch face from a department or discount store, measure carefully between the casings for the spring attachment. Most are 12–14mm, but they may be set too deeply for some of the larger, more decorative watch attachments to be inserted. The three-strand bead bar I used has a small profile that will fit most watch faces.

MATERIALS

- watch face
- 2 three-strand bead bar watch attachments (available at Fire Mountain Gems, www.firemountaingems.com or Jewels Express, www.jewelsexpress.com)
- 18 6mm round faceted quartz beads
- 18 4mm round faceted quartz beads
- 18 4mm disc-shaped faceted quartz beads
- 12 7mm lapis lazuli beads
- 6 cathedral beads
- toggle clasp
- 4 bead caps
- nylon bead cord, #3
- G-S Hypo Cement
- twisted wire beading needles

❶ Measure your wrist and add ½ in. (1.3cm) of ease for fastening the toggle clasp. To calculate the length of the beaded strands, measure the length of the watch face with the watch attachments. Subtract this amount and the length of the toggle from the total bracelet length. Divide by two to determine the length of each side.

❷ Cut three 12-in. (30cm) lengths of cord and insert one through each hole on the three-hole watch attachments. Tie them using a loose overhand knot (see "Basics," p. 9) so they won't slip back through the holes. You will untie this knot later to tighten and reknot the strands securely.

❸ When you design your strands, remember to start with small beads at the watch attachment and end with small beads at the bead cap. I used 4mm beads. My symmetrical, tapered design works well with a traditional watch face. However, a more random, casual design also works. To make your strands the right length, string the center strand, including both bead caps and two or three small beads before the clasp. These beads should be no larger than 6mm to permit the toggle to pivot and fit through the ring. When your bracelet design is the right length, remove the beads up to and including the bead caps. Then string the other two strands to match the beaded length of the middle strand.

❹ Once the three strands are the same length, thread the ends through the top of the first bead cap. Only one strand continues through the second bead cap. String two or three small beads no larger than 6mm and then the toggle or ring of the clasp. Go back through the small beads and the first bead cap **(photo a)**. The ends now come out between the two bead caps.

❺ Knot the strands tightly in a surgeon's knot (see "Basics") against the bead cap closest to the clasp **(photo b)**. Glue the knot. After the glue is dry, trim the ends and slide the other bead cap up to cover the knot.

❻ Push the beads on the three strands up against the bead cap. Untie the overhand knot. Tie two strands snugly

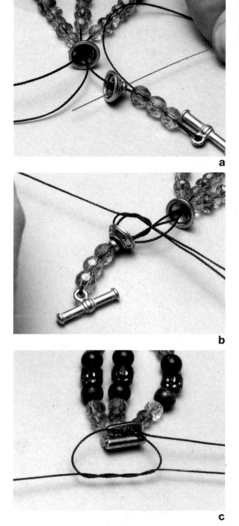

a

b

c

into a surgeon's knot against the watch attachment **(photo c)**. Tie the remaining strand and a strand tail from the first knot in another surgeon's knot. Glue the knots. After the glue is dry, trim the tails.

❼ Repeat steps 2–6 on the other side.

❽ Thread the springs from the watch face into the watch attachment and fit them into each side of the watch face.
– Emily Quinn

Easy multistrand
necklace

Pearls and summer parties go together like bubbles and champagne, but don't wait for a black-tie affair to show off this ensemble. Wear it whenever you feel like adding a touch of sophistication.

To make the necklace, string pearls of different colors—one color per strand, as shown here, or mix colors for confetti strands. Dress up the necklace with a ring or fob of crystals and pearls or other materials. I like to have more than one fob, switching them to match my mood or stringing multiples at one time. Set aside a few pearls for earrings. The

featured pair incorporates the same beads and techniques used to make the necklace. This project offers plenty of room for creative interpretation, so have fun making your own party pearls.

NECKLACE

❶ With 4 ft. (1.2m) of thread, tie a lark's head knot (see "Basics," p. 9 and photo a) on the clasp loop.
❷ Thread both ends through a needle and string three round spacer beads, a cylinder, and 15 in. (38cm) of pearls (photo b).
❸ String a cylinder, three round

spacers, and the other clasp half. Go back through one round spacer (photo c). Snug up the beads.
❹ Tie off the thread with a front-back-front knot as follows: Pull one thread out of the needle, and thread it through a second needle (figure 1). With a needle in each hand, tie half a square knot (see "Basics") in front of the pearl strand (figure 2). Turn the necklace over and repeat, tying the ends in the same order (right over left or left over right) as before. Turn the necklace over again and repeat to produce a third knot (figure 3).

a

figure 1   figure 2   figure 3

f

b

d

g

c

e

h

5 Sew both needles through the next spacer and repeat the three-knot process. Dab the knots with glue and let them dry. Go through the next few beads, and cut the threads.

6 Repeat steps 1-5, stringing five strands of pearls in total (photo d).

FOB

This ornamental ring dresses up the necklace, but it's optional.

1 Make a wrapped loop (see "Basics") on one end of the 24-gauge wire.

2 String 2½-3 in. (6-8cm) of pearls and crystals in an alternating pattern (photo e). Experiment with the length to make sure the ring slips over a clasp end and fits snugly around your pearls.

3 Start a wrapped loop close to the end bead and connect it to the first loop. Complete the loop (photo f). Trim the excess wire.

4 Slide the ring over the clasp's toggle end. Position the fob on the side or center of the necklace (photo g).

EARRINGS

1 Make a lark's head knot on the earring loop with 12 in. (30cm) of thread. String three round spacers.

2 String an alternating pattern of pearls and spacers. Then string three more round spacers (photo h).

3 Go through the earring loop and back through the first spacer. Make two front-back-front knots as before. Dab the knots with glue and let them dry. Go through the next spacer and cut the thread.

4 Make a second earring to match the first.
– *Diane Jolie*

MATERIALS

17-in. (43cm) necklace
- 5 16-in. (41cm) strands of pearls
- 30 2mm round spacer beads
- 10 5mm cylindrical spacer beads
- toggle clasp
- Fireline fishing line, 6-lb. test or Nymo D beading thread
- beading needles, #12
- G-S Hypo Cement

fob
- pearls left over from necklace
- 5-7 4mm crystals or fire-polished beads
- 7 in. (18cm) 24-gauge wire
Tools: wire cutters, roundnose and chainnose pliers

earrings
- pearls left over from necklace
- 32 2mm round spacers
- 2 earring wires
- Fireline fishing line, 6-lb. test or Nymo D
- beading needles, #12
- G-S Hypo Cement

Luxurious lariat

The best fringe benefit of owning a bead shop is that I can go wild when I choose beads for my designs. I came up with this lariat a few years ago and have returned to it many times because it's so versatile. When made with pearls, crystals, and a bevy of sparkling beads, it becomes a show-stopping, special occasion piece. To achieve a more casual look, tone it down with stone, ceramic, and matte-glass beads. Either way, you'll have a great time selecting the beads for its four generous strands.

First, select a focal bead to set the tone for the entire piece. I like to use an artist's bead like the dramatic ceramic cicada bead by Melanie Brooks above or the luscious, coral-colored glass bead by Blue Heeler at right. But faceted stones, carved bones, and wooden beads also make interesting and very affordable starting points. Don't choose a hollow or otherwise fragile bead, however, because it will not be sturdy enough to anchor the lariat.

Next, choose a hank of 11º seed beads in a color to coordinate with your focal bead. If the focal bead is monochromatic, choose seed beads in a contrasting color to set it off.

The fun but challenging part is selecting the 200-250 accent beads that give the lariat its luxurious appeal.

Don't be timid when choosing your accent beads. Look for variety in size, shape, and material. But stay within the color range determined by the focal bead and the seed beads. Keep in mind that the accent beads must be small enough to allow the lariat's four strands to slide easily through the end ring so stay within the 4-12mm size range.

For the coral and black lariat (below, right), I drew on the focal bead's dramatic colors, choosing a variety of black, salmon, and pink beads. I also looked for beads that drew the colors together, including vintage black and apricot marbleized glass beads and some clear Swarovski crystals with black swirls. I added pink pearls, matte-glass lampwork beads, and some enameled metal beads to complete the mix. For the cicada bead necklace, I drew from all the colors in the focal bead—gold, yellow, brown, and lots of green—and mixed them with the dark bronze of the seed beads.

Before you start stringing, decide on four accent beads or bead groups to end each strand. Go for something a little more dramatic than the other accent beads but harmonious enough not to compete or clash with the focal bead. After you've made one lariat, I'm sure you'll want to make other variations of this easy, eye-catching design.

❶ Cut two 6½-ft. (2m) lengths of flexible beading wire. Fold both wires in half and string 12-14 seed beads to the center of each wire.
❷ String one end of each wire through the ring. Adjust the number of seed beads so that the beaded section at each wire's center fits snugly around the ring.
❸ String all four wire ends through the focal bead or bead group and tighten against the seed beads (photo a).
❹ String four to five seed beads on one wire. Begin stringing the accent beads, separating them with seed beads. Make small patterns and repeats as you string, such as crystal, seed bead, crystal, seed bead, crystal or pearl, glass bead, pearl.
❺ When about 4 in. (10cm) of wire remain, string the accent bead or bead group chosen to end the strand and a crimp. String a seed bead or small bead,

MATERIALS

- 2.5-3.5cm focal bead
- stone, glass, or metal ring with a 1½ in. (4cm) opening
- hank size 11° seed beads
- 200-250 4-12mm accent beads, pearls, or crystals
- 14 ft. (4.2m) flexible beading wire, .014
- 4 crimp beads

Tools: diagonal wire cutters, crimping pliers

skip it, and bring the wire back through the crimp and several beads. Tighten so that the beads along the entire strand are snug. Crimp the crimp bead (photo b) and trim the excess wire.
❻ Repeat steps 4-5 with the other three strands. String one strand at a time, arranging the accent beads so they are offset from one another between the strands (photo c). Don't make all the strands exactly the same length. Vary the lengths 1-3 in. (3-8cm) to add interest when the necklace is worn.
❼ You can wear this lariat many different ways. To drape it as on p. 32, wrap two strands around your neck in one direction and two strands in the other direction, center the focal bead, and thread the four ends through the ring. You can try these other ways or create your own: wrap the lariat around your neck once or twice like a scarf, use it as a belt, or wear it with the focal bead at the back if you're wearing an open back dress.
– Irina Miech

a

b

c

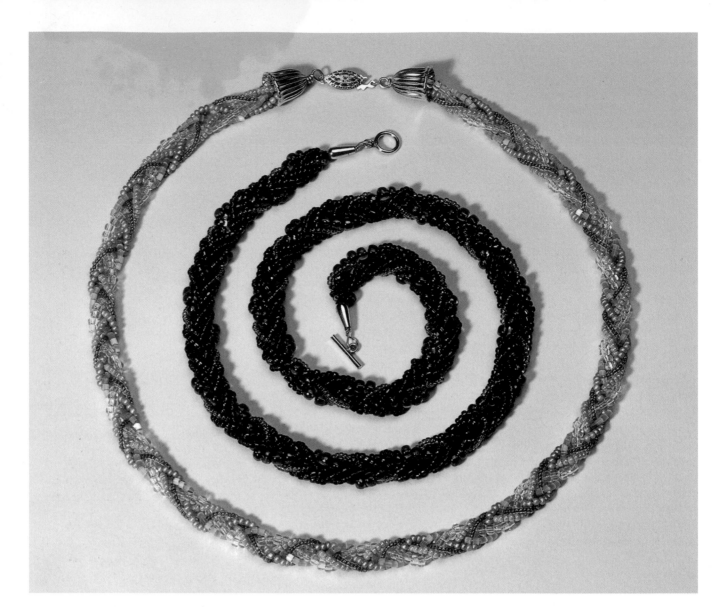

Braided five-strand necklace

After I'd agreed to fix a friend's braided necklace, I got busy trying to figure out how to do it. Several trials later, I returned the necklace fully repaired and found myself hooked on braiding.

I found several braiding patterns in craft books. You can use braiding to create a lariat-style necklace, a shorter necklace, or a bracelet. When picking beads for a necklace or bracelet, remember that variations in bead size from one strand to another will create unique and beautiful effects in the finished piece.

The directions that follow are for a 20-in. (51cm) necklace. To change the length of the necklace, use the following formula: Determine the desired length. Subtract 2 in. (5cm) for the clasp (the result is the finished length of the beaded section). Add one third of this number to itself (this is the length of each bead strand). Finally, add 10 in. (25cm) to this number. Now cut the strands to this length.

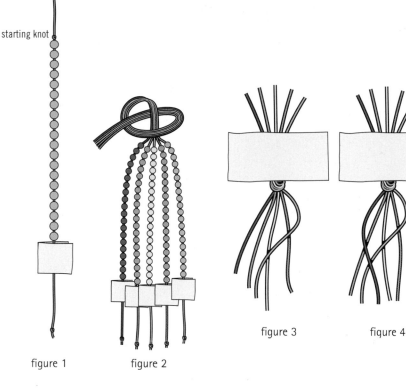

starting knot

figure 1   figure 2

figure 3   figure 4

the center strand (**figure 4**). Repeat figures 3 and 4 until the braid is the desired length.

You might want to wind long bead strands on bobbins to minimize tangling while you work: Make a bobbin by wrapping the beads around a card or piece of cardboard. If necessary, put the bobbin in a plastic bag to prevent it from unwinding.

Especially at the beginning, be sure you are braiding beads, not just thread. If the beads aren't part of the braid by the third iteration of the pattern, they are too loose on the thread. Slide the masking tape higher on the strand to tighten the beads.

As the braid progresses, a strand may become tighter than it was at the beginning. If this happens, slide the tape down slightly to add a little slack to the strand. Only do this to one or two strands at a time and add only about ¼ in. (6.5mm) of slack at a time. If you add too much slack, you will again be braiding thread and not beads.

❺ When the braid is the desired length, tie off as follows (an extra pair of hands is helpful for this step): Firmly grip the end of the braid and don't let go until you're done tying off. This will minimize the amount of the braid that loosens or unravels during the tying off process. Cut the ending knot off of each strand, slide the masking tape off the end of the thread, and remove any extra seed beads.

❻ Tie an overhand knot to hold all the strands together. Be sure the knot is tight against the end of the braid.

❼ Let go of the braid. If the end of the braid has loosened a bit, work the slack back up into the braid to even the braid tension.

❽ Cut 6 in. (15cm) of 20-gauge wire in half. With one piece of wire, make a wrapped loop (see "Basics") on one end.

❾ Tie one end of the necklace to the loop several times (**photo a**). Secure with clear nail polish.

❿ String a cone and make another wrapped loop through step 3. String half the clasp on the loop and finish the wrap (**photo b**). Trim the excess wire.

⓫ Repeat steps 8–10 on the other end.
– *Virginia Tutterow*

❶ Cut five 34-in. (86cm) lengths of thread. Tie a large overhand knot 5 in. (13cm) from one end of each strand (see "Basics," p. 9).

❷ Using only one type of seed bead, string 24 in. (61cm) of beads on one strand. Tie a knot at the very end of the strand so the beads do not slip off. Push the beads firmly toward the other end of the strand and hold them there with a piece of masking tape. The tape should be on the thread only, not on the beads (**figure 1**). Repeat for the remaining strands, using a different bead each time.

❸ Tie all the strands together at their starting knots with an overhand knot

(**figure 2**). Put a T-pin through the center of the overhand knot to slide it to the correct position before tightening the knot.

❹ Use masking tape to secure the top of the strands on a tabletop or a T-pin to pin the work to a board. Separate the strands in your hands, holding them near the top. Braid, keeping a light tension: take the right-hand strand over two strands so it becomes the center strand (**figure 3**). Take the left-hand strand over two strands so it becomes

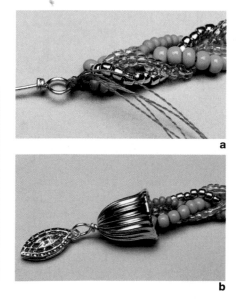

a

b

MATERIALS

- 5 kinds of seed beads, size 8º to 14º, coordinating colors
- Silamide beading thread
- beading needles, #12
- masking tape
- 2 cones
- 6 in. (15cm) 20-gauge wire
- clasp
- clear nail polish

Tools: roundnose and chainnose pliers, diagonal wire cutters

Finishing touches

Whether you're a jewelry designer or just have a passion for making your own jewelry, you've probably experienced the same frustration I do. The necklace is gorgeous, but where can you find a clasp that does it justice? Sometimes I create my own findings, but I've discovered that recently more and more designers are creating wonderful findings. For this necklace, I've used inlaid cones and a matching toggle

clasp by my friend and supplier Kelly Charveaux of Scottsdale Bead Supply (www.scottsdalebead.com). Many of the new designer clasps are so pretty that they can be used as a focal point, which means that a necklace can be worn in several different ways.

I was introduced to the world of gemstones and minerals 30 years ago and have gone from pet rocks and tumbled stones on macramé to faceting

my own gemstones and designing jewelry. I thought I wouldn't find any new interests, but then I took a colored stone class and discovered beads and pearls. I haven't been the same since.

DESIGN STRATEGIES

When I start a design, I consider two basic elements: harmony and balance. First, I develop a blend of harmonious colors. As I work toward completion, balance plays an increasing role. I like my designs to have an elegant simplicity and add interest through texture. Since I want my jewelry to be worn, comfort and fit are also important considerations. I love to create multistrand necklaces because I can incorporate a wonderful variety of elements.

If you free your imagination and persevere, new designs will come to you more and more easily. Next time you begin a design, choose the clasp first and use it to guide all your other choices.

NECKLACE CONSTRUCTION

❶ Cut five strands of flexible beading wire, each about 24 in. (61cm) long. I cut beading wire a little long to allow for design changes like braiding or twisting.

❷ String about 12 in. (30cm) of pearls to the center of each of the wires. Reserve two small pearls.

❸ String all five wires at one end of the necklace through a 12mm flat spacer, a 15mm accent bead, a 12mm flat spacer, and an 8mm flat spacer (photo a).

❹ Thread on a 3-to-1 multi-hole finding with the single hole toward the pearls, two wires through each of the outer holes, and one wire through the center hole (photo b).

❺ String a pattern of 4mm daisy spacers and two of the 5mm accent beads on the center wire, centering a reserved pearl. On each of the paired wires, string 4mm spacers, centering a 5mm accent bead. Add or remove daisy spacers to make all three strands the same length. String another 3-to-1 finding with all five wires exiting the single hole (photo c).

❻ String a crimp on each wire and thread the tail back through the crimp toward the beads, forming a small loop just large enough to accommodate the 18-gauge wire. Even up the loops and crimp tightly with crimping pliers (see "Basics," p. 9) or by mashing the crimp flat with chainnose pliers. Cut off all but a short tail of wire and feed each of the tails back into the single hole of the 3-to-1 finding.

❼ Cut the 18-gauge wire into two 3-in. (7.6cm) lengths. Start a wrapped

MATERIALS

- 4 16–18-in. (41–46cm) strands of 5–8mm pearls (here top-drilled freshwater pearls)
- 4 12–13mm flat sterling spacer beads
- 2 15–18mm disk-shaped accent beads
- 2 8–9mm flat sterling spacer beads
- 4 3-to-1 multi-hole sterling findings
- 60–80 4mm sterling daisy spacers
- 8 5mm sterling accent beads
- 2 5mm sterling daisy beads
- 10 ft. (3m) flexible beading wire, .012–.014
- 6 in. (15cm) 18-gauge sterling wire, half hard
- 10 crimp beads
- 2 inlaid sterling cones to match pearls
- matching inlaid sterling toggle and ring clasp

Tools: roundnose and chainnose pliers, wire cutters

Optional: crimping pliers

loop (see "Basics") about ¾ in. (2cm) from one end of a wire piece, thread on all five of the beading-wire loops (photo d), and make a single wrap with the wire tail. Trim the short tail.

❽ Thread a 5mm daisy spacer on the wire and thread the wire into one of the cones, pulling it down to cover the bundle of loops. String a 4mm daisy spacer to cover the hole at the top of the cone (photo e).

❾ Start a wrapped loop just above the spacer bead, thread on one part of the toggle clasp, and complete the wrapped loop. Trim the tail close and press it in with chainnose pliers (photo f).

❿ Repeat steps 3–9 on the other end of the necklace. Make sure that the pearls are snug before crimping in step 6. – Andrea Meloon

a

b

c

d

e

f

Leather cord necklace

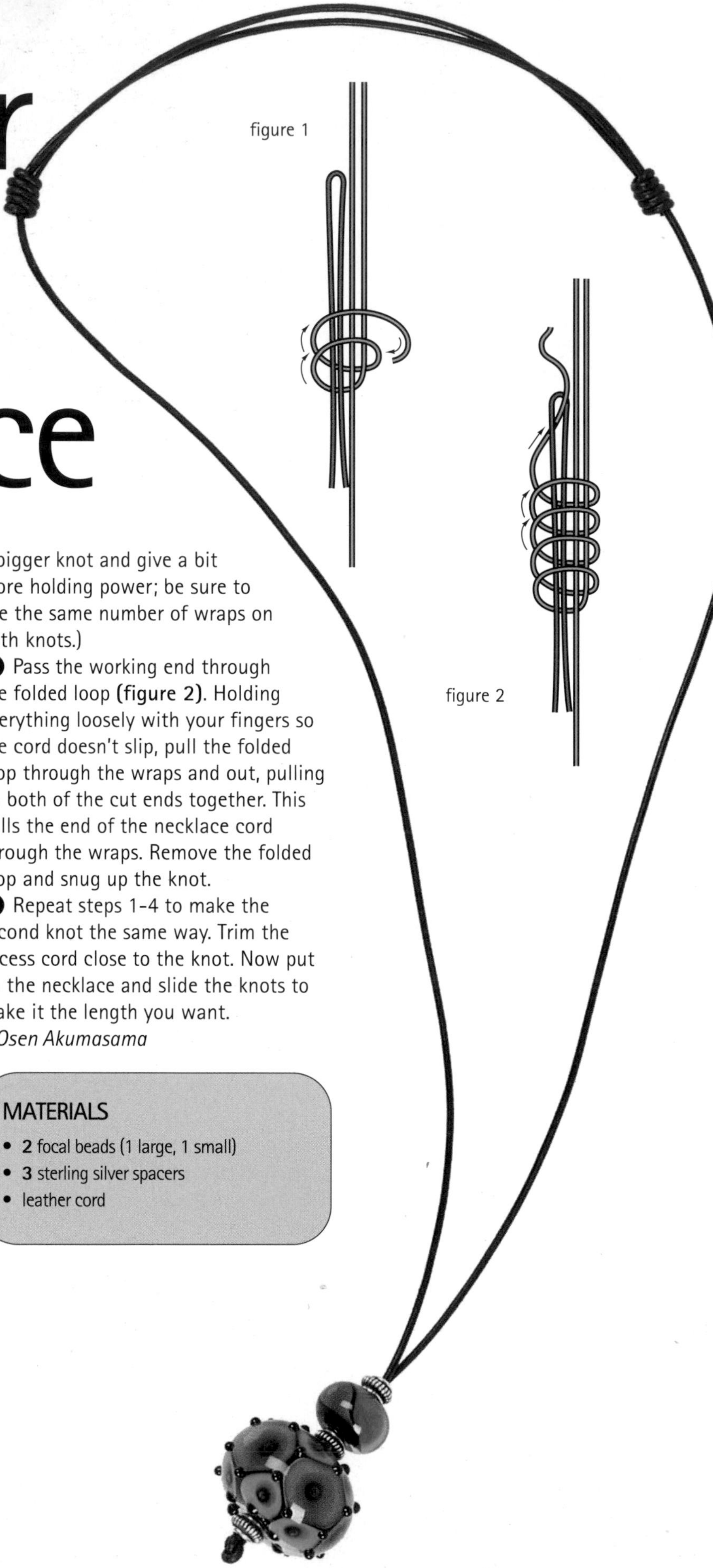

I often see beautiful lampwork beads strung simply on a leather cord, but sometimes the treatment doesn't do the beads justice. Here's a simple way to do it right.

STRING THE FOCAL BEADS

❶ Choose leather cord that's thin enough to go through the beads doubled. Then cut it the length of the planned necklace plus about 18 in. (46cm).

❷ Tie a knot in the middle of the cord—any kind will do, simple or decorative. (If you wish, skip the knot. String a small stopper bead and fold the thong in half over that bead instead.)

❸ Fold the cord in half at the knot and string a sterling silver spacer, a large focal bead, a spacer, a smaller focal bead, and another spacer over the doubled cord and down to the knot.

MAKE THE SLIDING KNOTS

❶ Overlap the ends of the cord by about 12 in. (30cm).

❷ Fold a 6-in. (15cm) piece of scrap cord in half and lay it on the overlapped cords about 3 in. (8cm) from one of the cut ends, with the loop end pointing away from the beads. Tape them down if you like.

❸ Pick up the 3-in. end of single cord (not the doubled scrap) and wrap it back around itself, the cord length, and the scrap piece of cord (figure 1), in the direction of the loop. It will wrap around four strands of thong. Make three to five wraps. (More wraps make

a bigger knot and give a bit more holding power; be sure to use the same number of wraps on both knots.)

❹ Pass the working end through the folded loop (figure 2). Holding everything loosely with your fingers so the cord doesn't slip, pull the folded loop through the wraps and out, pulling on both of the cut ends together. This pulls the end of the necklace cord through the wraps. Remove the folded loop and snug up the knot.

❺ Repeat steps 1-4 to make the second knot the same way. Trim the excess cord close to the knot. Now put on the necklace and slide the knots to make it the length you want.

– Osen Akumasama

figure 1

figure 2

MATERIALS

- **2** focal beads (1 large, 1 small)
- **3** sterling silver spacers
- leather cord

WIREWORK

Head pin earrings

HEAD PIN EARRINGS

❶ Put the bead or beads for the earring on a head pin (a wire rod with a small flattened end like the head of a sewing pin). The bottom bead goes on the pin first and the top bead last (**photo a**).

❷ Make a loop at the top of a head pin (see "Basics," p. 9 and **photo b**).

❸ Open the loop sideways (see "Basics") and attach it to the loop of an earring wire. Make the other earring to match the first.

JOINTED EYE PIN EARRINGS

❶ String the bead or beads that you want to have at the top of your earring on an eye pin. Make a loop at the other end of the eye pin.

❷ String the bead or beads you want to let dangle on a head pin, bottom bead first. Make a loop at the top.

❸ Assemble the earring by opening the loop at the top of the head pin and hooking it to the loop at the bottom of the eye pin. Close this loop. Then open the loop at the top of the eye pin, hook it to the loop on the earring finding, and close it.

Note: To open and close loops, bend the ends apart sideways. Never pull them away from each other because this fatigues the metal and will cause it to break. Support the closed side of the loop at the right angle and grasp the open side with the chainnose pliers. Then either pull it toward or away from yourself to make an opening large enough to attach the other loop. Close it by twisting the open end back into position. – Louise Malcolm

If you've got ten minutes and a few beads, you can make a beautiful pair of earrings with just one simple technique. String the beads on a head pin, turn a loop, attach it to an earring wire, and— *voilá!*—custom-made earrings are yours.

Make your earring slightly more complex by adding a second bead or bead group between the head pin group and the earring hook. This design allows for extra swing and movement, bringing playfulness to your earring wardrobe.

For this you need an eye pin, which is just like a head pin except that it has a loop on the end instead of a head. Whichever style you choose, you'll find unlimited possibilities in these two easy designs.

The critical technique for both of these earrings is the plain wire loop. An ideal loop is round and sits precisely above the bead like a balloon on a string. Don't worry if your first loops aren't great; practice makes perfect. But start out with inexpensive craft or copper wire before moving on to precious metal wire.

You can make small loops if you form them closer to the tips of the pliers and larger loops if you hold the wire where the jaws are thicker. It's a good idea to mark your pliers with the exact place to grip the wire for a ⅜-in. loop until you know it instinctively.

MATERIALS

- 2 of each kind of bead (**4** if you put 2 of the same bead in one earring)
- 2 head pins
- 2 eye pins (if making jointed earrings)
- 2 earring wires

Tools: chainnose and roundnose pliers, diagonal wire cutters

a   b

Dangles and drops

Hoop earrings with multiple, interchangeable dangles are easy to make and strike many moods. Combine crystal dangles with large hoops for evening glamour or gemstones, glass, and Bali silver with medium-sized silver hoops for a more casual look.

Make sure the hoops aren't too wide—the dangles must slide freely. To prevent the dangles from sliding off, the hoops should be a complete circle or nearly so. After picking hoops, the beads are easy.

1 For each dangle, string the bead(s) in order from bottom to top on a head pin.
2 Make a loop above the top bead of each dangle (see "Basics," p. 9).
3 With chainnose pliers, open a jump ring (see "Basics"), attach the dangles, close the ring, and slip it onto the loop.

Alternatively, omit the jump rings, as in the crystal earrings at right. For the long dangles, string the beads on a head pin and make a large wrapped loop above the top bead (see "Basics"). For each of the smaller dangles, string beads on a head pin and make a loop. Connect two dangles and slide them onto the hoop. – *Linda Salow*

MATERIALS

pearl earrings (photo a)
- 8 6mm pearls
- 32 4mm pearls
- 24 3mm gold beads
- 40 gold head pins
- 12 6mm jump rings
- 2 gold hoop earrings

silver and gemstone earrings (photo b)
- 4 11mm Bali beads
- 16 6mm glass and/or gemstone beads
- 8 3.5mm silver spacers
- 12 silver head pins
- 4 6mm jump rings
- 2 8mm jump rings
- 2 silver hoop earrings

crystal earrings (above)
- 2 12mm round crystals
- 10 4mm bicone crystals
- 11 4mm disc-shaped gold spacers
- 14 2mm gold beads
- 10 head pins
- 2 gold hoop earrings

gemstone chip earrings (inset above)
- 36 gemstone chips
- 18 4mm fire-polished beads
- 18 silver head pins
- 6 6mm jump rings
- 2 small silver hoop earrings

Tools: roundnose and chainnose pliers, diagonal wire cutters

a

b

Victorian tassels

This set of earrings offers a refined look with vintage flair. The dangles fall gracefully, enhancing both short or long hairstyles. Perfect for beginner or intermediate beaders, this two-hour project uses easy wirework techniques. Select a pair of filigree bead caps that have openings for attaching the dangles. Also make sure to use thin or small-gauge head and eye pins that will fit through the pearls' holes.

String the central dangle on a finding, and then connect the outer dangles to the bead cap.

1 String a 4mm crystal, a bead cap, and a 4mm crystal on an eye pin (**photo a**). Make the first half of a wrapped loop (see "Basics," p. 9), attach the finding, and finish the wrap (**photo b**).
2 String a 4mm crystal on an eye pin. Trim the wire to ³/₈ in. (1cm) and make a plain loop (see "Basics" and **photo c**).
3 String an 8mm crystal, a spacer, and a pearl on a head pin. Make a plain loop (**photo d**). Connect the three sections

to form the center dangle (**photo e**).
4 String a 4mm crystal, a spacer, and a 4mm crystal on an eye pin, and then make a plain loop (**photo f**). String a 4mm crystal, spacer, and a pearl on a head pin, then make a plain loop (**photo g**). Connect the two sections (**photo h**). Make a total of six dangles.
5 Hook a dangle on the edge of a bead cap (**photo i**). Continue until all dangles are attached (**photo j**).
6 Make a second earring to match the first. – *Iris Sandkühler*

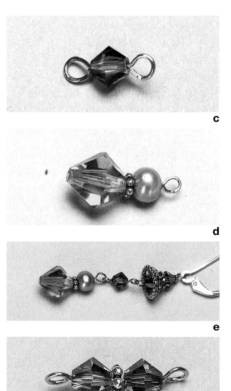

c

d

a

b

e

f

g

h

i

j

MATERIALS

- 42 4mm Swarovski bicone crystals
- 2 8mm Swarovski bicone crystals
- 14 4–5mm freshwater pearls
- 28 4mm daisy spacers
- 16 2-in. (51mm) small-gauge (22- or 24-gauge) eye pins
- 14 1-in. (25mm) small-gauge (22- or 24-gauge) head pins
- 2 filigree bead caps
- 2 earring findings

Tools: roundnose and chainnose pliers, diagonal wire cutters

Delicate flower earrings

If you want a delicate, elegant earring without lots of frill, try these. The blank earring wire (no loop) by TierraCast can be purchased at your local bead store or you can make it yourself as described in step 1, below.

❶ Cut a 2½-in. (6.4cm) piece of 20-gauge wire. Shape it as shown in **photo a**, using a cylindrical object, like a marker, to make the curve.

❷ String a bead cap and a 6mm bead on the long end of the wire. Trim the wire to ³⁄₁₆ in. (5mm). Then fold the wire over on itself with the tip of your chainnose pliers **(photo b)**. Use a metal file to smooth the end of the wire before you put it in your earlobe. – *Joanne Green*

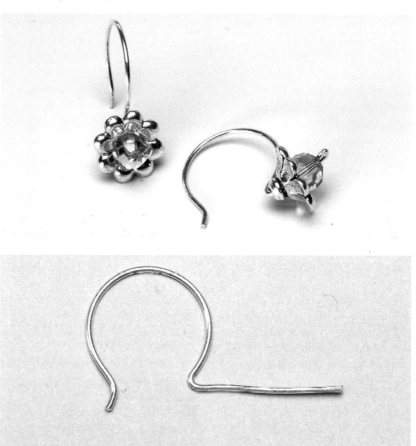

a

b

MATERIALS

- 2 blank earring wires (no loops) or 5 in. (13cm) 20-gauge sterling silver wire
- 2 bead caps
- 2 6mm beads

Tools: chainnose pliers, diagonal wire cutters, metal file

Antique button bracelet

A stash of vintage buttons and a recent acquisition of jump rings stirred my creative juices. I set out to design a bracelet that blends old and new materials yet preserves the buttons' integrity by not removing the shanks. Since the antique buttons are honored, this project appeals to seasoned button collectors as well as beaders. You can easily complete a bracelet in an hour—great for beginner and intermediate jewelry makers.

Construct the bracelet by threading pairs of seed beads on jump rings, then add alternating crow roller beads and buttons. I don't recommend glass crow rollers from India because they have inconsistencies. Pressed glass beads are best. This pattern makes a 7½-inch (19cm) bracelet, but you can increase or decrease the material counts to vary the length: Add or subtract groups of one button, two jump rings, eight seed beads, and one crow roller bead. If you use larger beads than I did, incorporate larger jump rings as well.

I like to flatten the button shanks slightly so the buttons lie flat against my wrist. This optional step (photo a) can be done by inserting chainnose pliers into a shank and squeezing until it becomes flat. Repeat with all buttons. Most of the bracelet's materials are readily available at local craft and bead stores or you can purchase kits directly from me.

❶ Open one jump ring with chainnose pliers (see "Basics," p. 9).
❷ Slide the following onto the jump ring: two seed beads, lobster claw clasp, two seeds, and one crow roller bead. Close the jump ring as shown in "Basics."

To close a jump ring securely, pull and push the ends back into the plane and continue a little past closed. Then jiggle them back to meet exactly. This helps harden the metal so the ring is less likely to pull open.
❸ Slip a second jump ring through the first crow roller. Add two seeds on each side of the open ring. Keep the ring open (photo b).
❹ Grip one end of the open ring with chainnose pliers. Slip a button onto the other end of the open ring, so that the button faces up and the clasp faces down. Close the ring with another pair of chainnose pliers or the tip of roundnose pliers held with your other hand (photo c).
❺ Open another jump ring. Slip it through the first button shank. Add two seeds on each side of the ring (photo d) then a crow roller. Hold the ends of the ring with both pliers and close it.
❻ Repeat steps 3-5 until you've attached the last crow roller bead. Close the ring.
❼ Slip the final jump ring through the last roller bead and close it. Use this ring as the other clasp end. – Candace Silber

MATERIALS
- 9 antique or new metal buttons, approx. ½-in. (1.3 cm) diameter with thin wire shanks
- 20 9mm jump rings, 19-gauge
- 76 size 6º Japanese seed beads
- 10 6mm crow roller beads
- lobster claw clasp, medium

Tools: roundnose and chainnose pliers or two pair of chainnose pliers

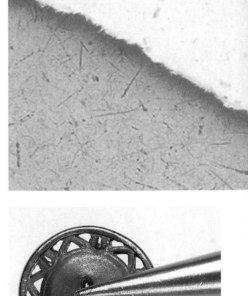

a

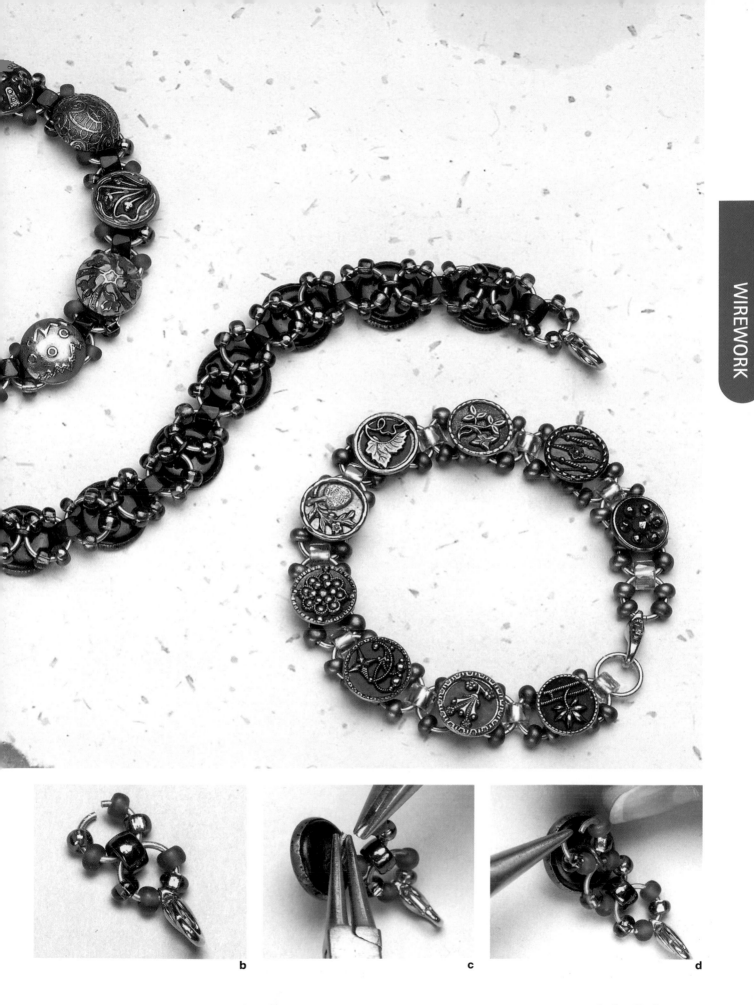

b

c

d

Embellished
bead chain

Delicate necklaces never go out of style. They make us look and feel feminine and pretty. This update of a classic Victorian look is a chain of beaded units, each joined with a single link. It adds color and sparkle near the face, but it still has the light, airy look of a chain necklace. The necklace's length is adjustable so that it can range from a classic choker of approximately 14 in. (36cm) to a neckline length of 18 in. (46cm). The three-bead motif is echoed in the matching earrings.

This necklace is easy to make because you use only one technique; however, that technique—wrapped loops—requires practice. It's a good idea to practice with base metal head pins or copper wire before you begin using sterling silver or gold-filled head pins.

The most important thing to remember about wrapped loops is that once they've been wrapped, you can't open them to attach them to other loops. Therefore, you must attach them before wrapping. You will probably forget once or twice, but one of the great things about this design is that all the elements join with split rings. Thus, you can still slip the ring onto the loop if you complete the wrap too soon.

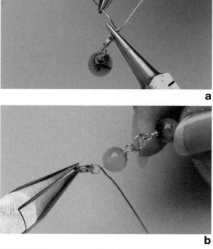

NECKLACE

❶ Begin at the back with the adjustable-length bead chain section: Put a large crystal on a head pin. Make the first half of a wrapped loop (see "Basics," p. 9). Slide a split ring into the loop and complete the wrap.

❷ Cut a 3-in. (7.6cm) piece of wire, make the first half of a wrapped loop, slide the split ring from the last step into the loop, and finish the wrap (photo a). String a large bead and begin another wrapped loop above it. Before wrapping, link it to a split ring (photo b). Repeat this step twice more.

❸ Now begin the three-bead units: thread a large bead on a head pin and make a wrapped loop above it. Cut a 4-in.-long (10cm) piece of wire and begin a wrapped loop. Link it to the split ring at the end of the bead chain and complete the wrap. Thread a large bead on the wire, then the loop of the bead on the head pin, and finally another large bead (photo c). Begin

a wrapped loop and connect it to a split ring before wrapping.

❹ Repeat step 3 15 more times to connect 16 bead units. End the necklace by attaching a large bead to the last split ring with a wrapped loop as in step 2. Begin the second loop, attach the hook, and complete the wrap (photo d).

❺ To perfect the way the necklace hangs, correct the alignment of each pair of loops. Hold one loop with roundnose pliers. Grasp the other loop with chainnose pliers and rotate both pliers until the loops are in the same plane (photo e). The split rings will sit at a right angle to them.

❻ Finally, make 15 small-bead dangles on head pins. Attach each to the bottom of a split ring between three-bead units with a wrapped loop (photo f).

EARRINGS

❶ Cut two ¾ in. (2cm) pieces of chain. Make sure each piece has an odd number of links.

❷ Make two three-bead units as in step 3 of the necklace, but omit the split rings. Instead, before completing the side wraps, slide the end link of a

MATERIALS

16½ in. (42cm) necklace
- 53 6mm faceted round crystals
- 15 4mm faceted round crystals
- 32 small-gauge (22- to 24-gauge) sterling silver head pins
- 5mm sterling silver split rings
- 6 ft. 24-gauge sterling silver wire
- sterling silver hook clasp

earrings
- 6 6mm faceted round crystals
- 2 small-gauge (22- to 24-gauge) sterling silver head pins
- 4 in. (10cm) 24-gauge sterling silver wire
- 2 earring wires

Tools: chainnose and roundnose pliers and wire cutters; split ring pliers optional

piece of chain into the loop. Complete the wraps.

❸ Open the loop (see "Basics") of an earring wire and attach the middle link of one piece of chain. Close the loop. Repeat with the other earring wire.
– *Nicolette Stessin*

Charm bracelet

Lampwork beads attract attention. The fun shapes and colors catch everyone's eye. Transform these beads into dangles by adding crystals and decorative wrapped loops to create a colorful charm bracelet.

Rollo chain has links at right angles to each other and every other link is on the same plane (photo a). The dangles need to be attached to links on the same plane, or the chain will twist and the bracelet will be uncomfortable to wear. Attach the first dangle to the end link of chain and skip an odd number of links between each dangle. Select lampwork beads and crystals with contrasting colors.

❶ String a crystal, a lampwork bead, and a crystal on each head pin. Arrange the head pin components in the order they will be attached to the chain (photo b).

❷ Cut a 3½-in. (9cm) length of wire. Grasp the center of the wire with the chainnose pliers and bend it into a right angle. Make the first half of a wrapped loop (see "Basics," p. 9). Slide the loop through the end link of chain and complete the wrap with two or three wraps.

❸ String a crystal on the wire and make the first half of a wrapped loop. This loop should be in the same plane as the first loop and close to the crystal. Slide the loop through the loop on the toggle (photo c). Complete the wrap.

❹ To determine the length of chain you need, subtract the length of the clasp and crystal links from the desired length of the bracelet. Or place the chain around your wrist and find the point where the chain crosses the end of the clasp. Cut the chain at that point. Make sure the end link is oriented in the same plane as the other end link.

❺ Repeat steps 2 and 3 with the remaining wire and clasp part at the other end of the chain.

❻ Working from one end of the chain to the other, attach the head pin components. Make the first half of a wrapped loop directly above and close to the crystal of the first head pin component. Attach the loop to the last link of chain (where the crystal is connected). Complete the wrap.

❼ Connect the remaining head pin components to the chain, leaving five links between each dangle (photo d).
– *Irina Miech*

a

b

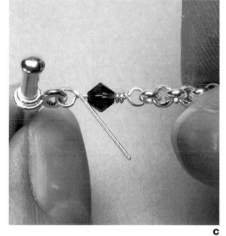

c

MATERIALS

- 10–15 lampwork beads (alphabet beads by Jamie Dierks, jamiesstudio.com)
- 22–32 4mm bicone crystals
- 10–15 2-in. (5cm) 24-gauge (fine) sterling silver head pins
- 7 in. (18cm) 22-gauge sterling silver wire, half-hard
- 5–7 in. (13–18cm) rollo chain
- toggle clasp

Tools: chainnose and roundnose pliers, wire cutters

d

Crystal slide necklace

My daughter and I enjoy shopping at the mall. Every time without fail, we stop at her favorite jewelry boutique. And every time, without fail, she finds something that she just has to have. On the last trip, she found a pretty crystal choker—terribly overpriced for the quality, I thought. I knew that it would be a cinch to make and, of course, I promised I would. After a few slips, it went quickly, and she hasn't taken it off since.

Crystals provide an elegant touch to this design, but almost any small bead would work well. Large seed beads, small faceted stone beads, or ceramic beads would make fine substitutes as long as their holes were large enough to let them glide easily along the wire. Also, this design needn't be limited to choker

length. You could make a longer strand or even two graduated strands of these beaded links. The design is so playful it invites you to use your imagination and explore the possibilities.

❶ Cut the heads off the head pins or cut 17 3-in. (7.6cm) lengths of wire. I prefer to use head pins rather than wire because their strength and shortness make them easy to work with.

❷ Start a wrapped loop on one of the ends (see "Basics," p. 9). Add the split ring and complete the wrap. String two crystals. Make a wrapped loop ⅝ in. (1.6cm) from the first wrapped loop. Put it aside.

❸ Begin another wrapped loop on another head pin. Link it to the first component and finish the wrap. String

two crystals. Make a wrapped loop ⅝ in. from the first. Try to make sure all of your components are the same length.

❹ Repeat step 3 for a total of 17 components.

❺ Before finishing the last wrap on the last component, add the clasp. Finish the wrap. – *Linda Salow*

MATERIALS

15-in. (38cm) choker
- 34 4mm crystals or small beads
- 17 3-in. (7.6cm) sterling silver head pins or 5 ft. (1.5m) 20-gauge sterling silver wire
- sterling silver clasp
- sterling silver split ring

Tools: roundnose and chainnose pliers, wire cutters

Pearl drop necklace

The necklace above is a very straightforward take on combining chain and pearls. The concept is not new, but the types of chain now available—small links, large links, various size links— makes it enticing. Pearls, too, are available in many colors, shapes, and sizes. Faceted, coin-shaped, disc-shaped, even cross-shaped pearls are on the market.

❶ String a silver bead, a pearl, and a silver bead on a head pin. Make the first half of a wrapped loop (see "Basics," p. 9). Make three more "A" components.

❷ String a silver bead and a pearl on a head pin. Make the first half of a

wrapped loop. Make two more "B" components like this one.

❸ Cut the head off of a head pin and make the first half of a wrapped loop on one end. String a silver bead, a pearl, and a silver bead. Begin a wrapped loop on the other end. Repeat to make three more "C" components.

❹ Find the central link on your chain. Connect a "C" component to this link, and finish the wrap (see "Basics"). Connect another "C" and complete the wrap. Add a "B" at the bottom and complete the wrap.

❺ Place the remaining components along the chain and determine the most appealing order for linking them. When

MATERIALS

- 11 4–5mm freshwater pearls
- 19 2mm silver beads
- 18 in. (45cm) silver necklace
- 11 2 in. (5cm) sterling silver head pins (22- or 24-gauge)

Tools: roundnose and chainnose pliers, diagonal wire cutters

satisfied, link them to the chain. Before finishing the wraps, count to be sure you have the same number of links between the components on each side (if symmetry matters in your design).

– *Sue Raasch*

Coiled head pin earrings

Have you ever imagined a wonderful jewelry design, but then discovered you didn't have all the supplies you needed to make it? Or worse, that they didn't exist? When this happens, don't despair —just adapt the design to suit the supplies or transform available materials into the forms you desire. The earrings above are a perfect example of the second approach.

Usually when you make an earring, the beads hang on a head pin or an eye pin (or both). If you don't have an eye pin handy, it's easy to make one from a head pin simply by cutting off the head and making a loop. But how do you make an earring if you're out of head pins since you need a way to prevent beads from falling off the wire?

One desperate evening with no head pins in sight, I tried coiling up the straight end of an eye pin to secure the beads as a head pin would. I was so pleased with the resulting shape, a tightly coiled spiral, that it has become a staple in many of my designs. I don't

just use it for earrings. It's also wonderful for making bead pendants for necklaces.

❶ String the beads in your earring design on the eye pin. Remember, the eye on the pin will be at the top of the completed earring rather than at the bottom. This is the reverse of the order normally used.

❷ Use the very tip of your chainnose pliers to grasp the pin next to the last bead and bend it at a right angle

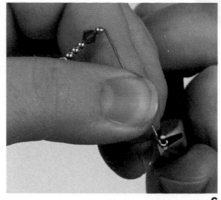

a

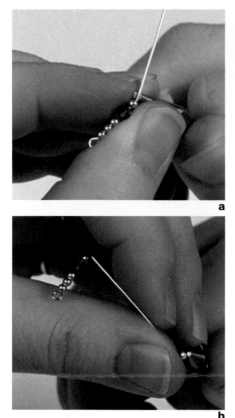

b

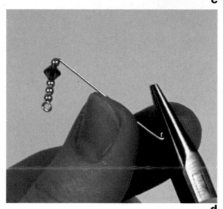

c

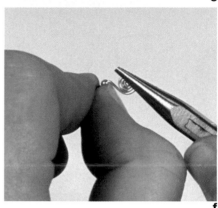

e

d

f

(photo a). If you grasp the pin further in on the jaws your angle won't be close enough to the bead for a snugly strung dangle.

❸ Use your roundnose pliers to begin the coil. Grasp the end of the pin with the very tip of the pliers. Roll it over to form a very small hook (photo b).

❹ Switch back to the flat pliers and squeeze the hook to compact it (photo c).

❺ Now grasp the hook flat in the jaws of the flat pliers. Pinching tightly to prevent it from turning, begin to bend the straight part of the pin around the hook. Use your thumb to force the pin to spiral around the previous revolution (photo d).

❻ After each bend, open the pliers

slightly and adjust the coil so you can continue to wrap the spiral (photo e).

❼ As you near the right angle, you may find it easier to grasp the coil with the pliers and turn the pliers to wrap the last part of the pin (photo f).

❽ Finally, use the flatnose or chainnose pliers to straighten and flatten the finished coil.

If you want a more handwrought look, use a ball-peen hammer to hammer the coils flat, but take care to avoid striking or breaking any of the beads. – *Sarah K. Young*

styling tips

• Try using niobium wire, which comes in bright colors that can add an interesting twist to a design. Be sure to wrap the tips of your pliers with masking tape, however, or you risk scratching the colored finish.

• When you use coils in your designs, pay attention to the direction they turn—clockwise or counterclockwise, depending on whether you look at them from one side or the other. Earrings look best if they're mirror images of each other so both coils should curve either toward or away from your face.

• If you put the coiled section in an upper portion of an earring, you may need to turn the eye at a right angle to the coil to make the coil hang facing the right direction (see photo below).

MATERIALS

• assorted beads
• 2 earring wires
• eye pins or wire (I usually use 22-gauge gold-filled or sterling silver, but sometimes only 24-gauge will go through semi-precious stones or pearls.) Each coil takes 1–1½ in. (2½–4cm).

Tools: roundnose and chainnose or flatnose pliers, diagonal wire cutters

Coiled wire bracelet

When I saw these beautiful, blue, faceted chalcedony beads, I just had to combine them with some elegant blue-gray keshi pearls I already had. The new blue topaz clasp was the perfect accompaniment for the bracelet. And for less than $150, I had a piece worthy of any high-end jewelry store. Of course you could substitute less expensive stones and pearls to make the initial investment less costly.

Choose relatively flat stones and pearls because the dense way these are strung through every link of chain makes for a thick bracelet that works out to be shorter than the length of the chain alone. The thicker your beads, the longer the chain you'll need to start with. Ideally, you should string the beads on the chain until it's long enough to go around your wrist comfortably before cutting it to the final length.

Add pearl and coil embellishment to every other link of the chain, starting and ending with the third link from each end. Then add a pair of gemstones to every other link, starting and ending in the second link from each end. Finally, attach a decorative clasp with small, heavy jump rings.

I used 2-in.-long (5cm) ball-end head pins for the chalcedony bracelet and 1½-in.-long (3.8cm) head pins for the appatite bracelet (at right). If you prefer, make your own head pins by bending the last ¹⁄₁₆ in. (1.5mm) of a piece of 22- or 24-gauge wire down against the length of wire (see "Basics," p.9 and **photo g**).

STARTING

For a bracelet that is ½ in. (1.3cm) longer than your wrist circumference, not counting the clasp, cut the chain 1½ in. (3.8cm) longer than your wrist circumference; or don't cut the chain until the bracelet length has been determined with the beads attached.

EMBELLISHMENT

❶ String a pearl on a ball-end head pin and thread the pin through the third link from one end of the chain. Bend the wire at a right angle ¹⁄₁₆ in. (1.5mm) on the other side of the link (**photo a**).

❷ Starting at the tip of the head pin wire, make a tiny loop with the tip of a roundnose pliers (**photo b**).

❸ Hold the loop with chainnose pliers and coil the wire around the loop (**photo c**). Reposition the pliers as needed to keep the coil flat and tight (**photo d**). Roll the coil up to the chain and bend it parallel to the pearl (**photo e**).

❹ Repeat steps 1-3 in every other link of the chain until you have gone through the third-to-the-last link. Be sure to put all the pearls on the same side of the chain.

❺ String a stone on a ball-end head pin and thread it through the second link of the chain. String on another stone and trim the head pin ⅛ in. (3mm) past the stone (**photo f**).

a

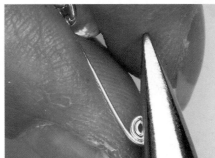

d

g

b

e

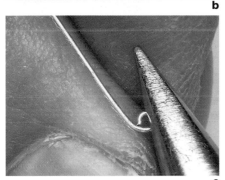

c

f

h

MATERIALS

- 70–80 4–5mm faceted stone rondelles
- 34–40 4–5mm keshi pearls
- 70–80 sterling head pins with ball head, 1½–2 in. (3.8–5cm) long, or 4½ yd. (4m) 24-gauge wire
- 7½–9½ in. (19–24cm) 4.5mm rollo or cable sterling chain
- 2 18-gauge 5mm jump rings
- Jeweled single-strand clasp with safety, ½-in.-long (1.3cm) (this one is from Pacific Silver works, (805) 641-1394, www.pacificsilverworks.com)

Tools: chainnose and roundnose pliers, diagonal wire cutters

6 Use the tip of your chainnose pliers to fold the last ¹⁄₁₆ in. down against the wire so it just touches the stone **(photo g)**.

7 Repeat steps 5-6 through every other link, ending with the next-to-last link. Put all the ball ends on the same side of the chain.

FINISHING

1 Open an 18-gauge jump ring side to side (see "Basics," p.9) or cut open a chain link for a jump ring. Pass the ring through the end link at one end of the bracelet and the loop on one part of the clasp **(photo h)**. Close the jump ring.

2 Repeat at the other end of the bracelet. – *Juana Jelen*

Elegant wire earrings

Here's a quick earring technique that you can use to show off a few favorite beads. The earrings on the left display Japanese miracle beads strung onto a central wire and surrounded with delicate wire S-curves.

The earrings at right feature Bali silver beads strung on a Bali head pin. For the S-curves on this pair, I used twisted wire, which provides a rope-like texture that complements the beads.

❶ String each head pin with the following sequence of beads: 2mm, 5mm, 7mm, 7mm, 5mm, and 2mm (photo a). You can use purchased head pins or make your own using 20-gauge wire (see "Basics," p. 9).

a

b

figure 1

figure 2

2 Cut two 2¼-in. (5.7cm) and two 2½-in. (6.4cm) lengths of either plain or twisted wire for the S-curves. Shape each of the longer pieces into an S-curve following **figure 1** in the template above. Bend the shorter wires into curves following **figure 2**.

3 Lay out the wires in two sets consisting of one short and one long "S" with the large curve on top **(photo b)**. Since the finished earrings will have a right- and left-hand orientation, make sure you arrange the sets so they are the mirror image of each other.

Working with one set of wires at a time, turn a small loop at the top and bottom of each piece. Turn each loop away from you and toward the curve in the "S."

4 Attach a shorter "S" to one of the beaded wires by hooking its lower loop below the last bead on the wire. Slip the "S" wire's upper loop between the top 7mm bead and the 5mm bead. Pinch the loops closed after you hook them onto the beaded wire. Keep the beaded head pin straight as you work.

5 Attach the lower loop of the longer "S" between the bottom 2mm and 5mm beads. Attach the upper loop between the top 5mm and the 2mm beads **(photo c)** or above the 2mm bead if that is an easier fit. Adjust the curves slightly with your fingers as you make these connections. The "S" wires should pass neatly between beads, touching the beaded head pin.

6 Make a plain or wrapped loop (see "Basics") at the top of the beaded head pin. Slip the loop onto an earring wire and close the loop. Adjust the "S" curves so they hang perpendicular to the ear wire.

7 Repeat, making the second earring the mirror image of the first.
– *Wendy Witchner*

c

MATERIALS

- 4 7mm round beads
- 4 5mm round beads
- 4 2mm sterling silver beads
- 6 in. (15cm) 20-gauge sterling silver wire or 2 3 in. (7.6cm) decorative Bali silver head pins
- 10 in. (25cm) 20- or 22-gauge round or twisted wire
- 2 sterling silver earring wires with loop

Tools: roundnose and chainnose pliers, wire cutters

Optional: hammer, anvil, and file

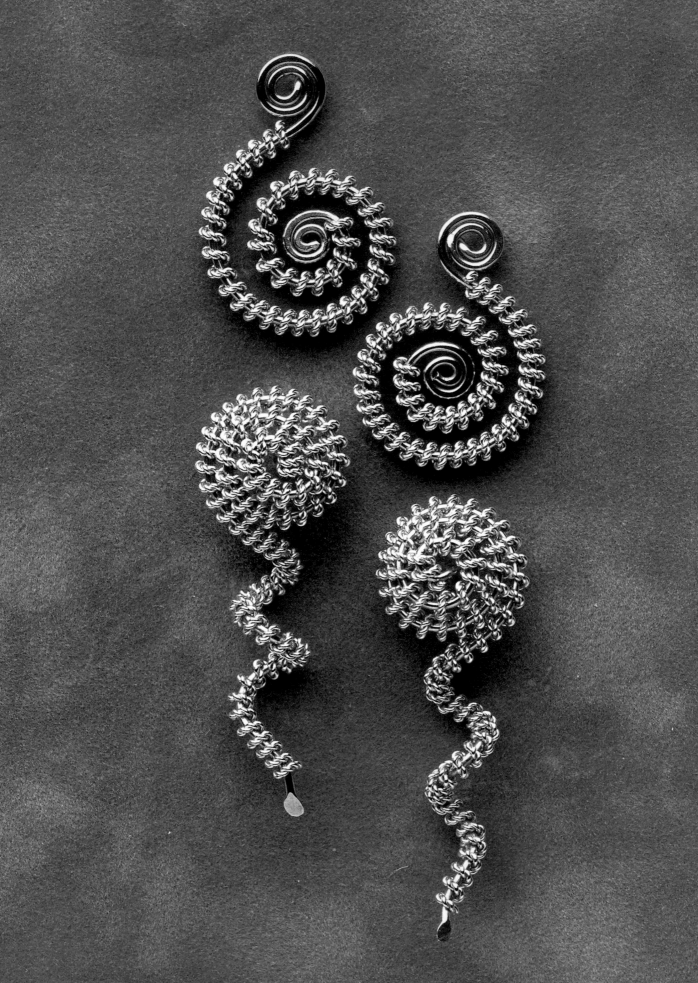

Two spiral earring styles

You can make these earrings with silver wire only or mix gold and silver together. Using two colors brings out the twist wire's texture, giving these earrings a filigree look.

Make both earrings simultaneously to ensure they match. When wrapping the twist wire, space the wraps out slightly so the thicker wire is visible between each wrap.

SCROLL EARRINGS (opposite, top)

❶ Cut two 5½-in. (14cm) lengths of 18-gauge wire. Trim the ends flush and file any sharp edges smooth.

❷ Wind the twist wire around the 18-gauge wires, covering 3 in. (8cm) on each one. Leave 1-2-in. (2.5-5cm) tails of twist wire unwrapped at each end.

❸ To form the earring posts, bend a right angle ½ in. (1.3cm) from the exposed end of each 18-gauge wire.

❹ Grasp the wire with roundnose pliers at the bend and use the chainnose pliers to roll it around the tip of the roundnose pliers (photo a). Turn two complete rotations. Turn the

spiral in the opposite direction on the second wire.

❺ Slide the twist-wire coils up to the spiral on each wire. Turn a spiral at the other end of each wire, rotating twice in the opposite direction (photo b).

❻ Hammer the spirals at both ends to flatten them.

❼ Use your hands to curve the wrapped wire into an expanding spiral around each earring's bottom spiral (the one without the post). Complete 1¾ turns around the central spiral. Keep the spirals in a single plane. Add or remove wraps as needed to cover the wire. Trim excess twist wire.

SWIRL EARRINGS (opposite, bottom)

❶ Cut two 6½-in. (16.5cm) lengths of 18-gauge wire. Prepare as in step 1 above.

❷ Make earring posts as in step 3 above.

❸ Wrap the twist wire around the 18-gauge wire from the post to ½ in. (1.3cm) from the end. Leave 1-2-in. tails of twist wire at each end.

❹ Slide the wrapped wire away from the post. Turn a spiral around the post as in step 4 above. After one turn, push the wrapped wire back around the turn to the earring post (photo c). Repeat with other wire, turning the spiral in the opposite direction.

❺ Bend each wire with your hands in an expanding spiral, fitting each rotation behind the previous one to form a dome around the earring post. Make three complete rotations on each earring.

❻ Using your hands or a mandrel (hanger wire is a good width), form loose corkscrew spirals with the remaining wire (photo d). Trim the exposed 18-gauge wire to ⅛ in. (3mm).

MATERIALS

scroll earrings
- 1 ft. (30cm) 18-gauge gold-filled or sterling silver wire
- 1 yd. (.9m) 24-gauge twisted silver wire
- 2 earring nuts or backs

swirl earrings
- 15 in. (38cm) 18-gauge gold-filled or sterling silver wire
- 40 in. (1m) 24-gauge twisted silver wire
- 2 earring nuts or backs

Tools: chainnose and roundnose pliers, diagonal wire cutters, file, hammer and anvil

a

b

c

d

Flatten the end with a hammer and file smooth. Adjust the wraps and trim the excess. – *Wendy Witchner*

Button bracelets

After taking Lynne Merchant's coiling bead workshop several years ago, I worked to develop my own style. At first I designed wire jewelry with lampworked glass beads; but when I met my friend and button dealer, Vicki Hanwell, I discovered cut-steel vintage buttons. I purchased a few to play with and soon became an addict.

You can make the bracelets shown here either with a round, flat lampworked bead or a button. Buttons or beads should have a diameter of 1 in. (2.5cm) or greater, and buttons need a metal shank because tightening the wire around a glass shank could break it.

MAKING THE BAND

❶ Cut a length of 14-gauge wire about an inch shorter than the circumference of your wrist. Wrap it about three-quarters of the way around your wrist, leaving the last $^1/_2$–$^5/_8$ in. (1.3-1.6cm) on each end straight (photo a, p. 62).

❷ Use roundnose pliers to make a loop in the twist wire that's just the right size to wrap the band tightly. Begin coiling the twist wire around the band, $^1/_2$–$^5/_8$ in. from the end. Hold the loop in place with chainnose pliers as you bend the wire around the band with your fingers (photo b, p. 62). Make sure it stays snug by squeezing periodically with the pliers. After about an inch, you won't need the pliers anymore.

You can coil tightly or leave gaps for a more textured effect. The length of twist wire you'll need depends on which wrap style you prefer and the gauge of the twist wire, but it will be approximately four to five times the length of the band. Stop coiling $^1/_2$–$^5/_8$ in. from the other end.

❸ Make a loop at one end of the band in the same plane (photo c, p. 62).

❹ Flatten the other end by placing it on the steel disk or anvil and hitting it with the hammer a few times. Then bend it backward to form a hook (photo d, p. 62).

FRAMING THE BUTTON

The gauge of wire you choose depends on the size of the button or bead and the number of circles you want to make around it. I usually make two circles and like to use 14-gauge wire. Make sure that your wire fits through the button shank or bead hole.

❶ Determine how much wire to cut by bending the wire into a circle that frames the bead or button. Cut a piece of wire four to five times that length.

❷ Use roundnose pliers to make a loop

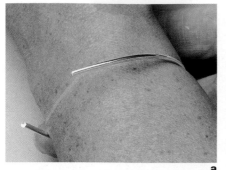

a

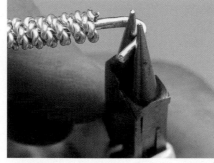

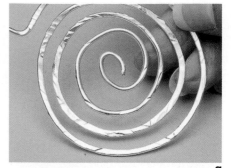

g

b

d

e

h

c

f

i

that will fit through the button shank. Set the button in place temporarily. Coil increasingly large circles (two to three) that will remain hidden behind the button to support it (photo e).

❸ When you reach the button's edge, make about two more increasingly large circles to frame the button. About ⅝ in. from the end of the wire bend it away from the coil at a right angle (photo f).

❹ Remove the button and hammer the coiled wire. Be careful not to flatten the wire on the ends and the two or so circles that will be hidden under the button (photo g). Using roundnose pliers, complete a loop with the outer end of the wire by rolling it upward so the loop is perpendicular to the coil.

❺ To attach the frame to the button, open the loop at the center of the coil and slip it on the shank. Close it as tightly around the shank as possible. Adjust the unflattened coils to wrap the shank securely at least once more and to support the button so it won't flop.

I use my chainnose pliers and fingers to make small adjustments while framing the wire to the button.

❻ Finally, attach the loop on the band to the loop on the frame (photo h).

FRAMING A BEAD

❶ Estimate the length of the bead hole and add ½ in. Then circle around this length of wire two to three times.

❷ Bend the bead-hole length of wire straight up so you won't hit it and flatten the coils.

❸ Bend the wire back down, insert the bead, and bend the end down perpendicular to the hole so the bead won't slip off (photo i). Complete with a loop at the other end of the frame (step 4 above). The bead shown is by Carolyn Driver of Blue Heeler Glass.

– Wendy Witchner

MATERIALS

- 36 in. (.9m) 14-gauge silver, gold-filled, or copper wire
- 36-48 in. (.9-1.2m) 18- or 20-gauge silver or gold-filled twist wire (note: 20-gauge twist wire is two pieces of 20-gauge wire twisted together to yield 16-gauge wire; 18-gauge yields 14-gauge twisted wire)
- round, flat bead or metal-shank button, 1 in. (2.5cm) diam. or larger

Tools: chainnose and roundnose pliers, sturdy diagonal wire cutters, hammer, and steel disk or anvil

Optional: liver of sulfur or antiquing agent (for finishing silver), 00 steel wool

STITCHING

Square stitch basics

Square stitch, a durable weave in which beads are aligned neatly in both vertical and horizontal rows, is one of the easiest stitches to learn. Many beaders like to use square stitch as an alternative to loom weaving because it produces the same look without numerous threads that have to be finished off. Because square stitch produces a nice even grid, it is particularly well-suited to Japanese cylinder beads, Other bead types work fine as well, especially if an uneven texture is desired.

BASIC SQUARE STITCH

❶ String the required number of beads for the first row. Next, string the first bead of the second row and go through the last bead of the first row and the bead just added in the same direction. The new bead sits on top of the old bead and the holes are parallel.

❷ String the second bead of row 2 and go through the bead below it. Continue through the bead just added. Repeat this step for the entire row and add more rows in the same manner.

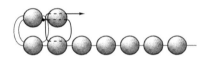

INCREASING SQUARE STITCH

To increase the width of your work by one bead, before starting the next row, add two beads. Go back through them both in the same direction and then resume working across the established row.

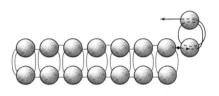

DECREASING SQUARE STITCH ALONG THE EDGE OF A ROW

If your design requires that your rows get narrower, you will need to decrease. To decrease the number of beads in a row of square stitch, backtrack through the next-to-last row, coming out the bead below where the new row will start. Go through the bead immediately above on the last row. Now begin the new row.

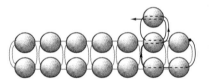

Reversible bracelets

I love triangle beads. Over the past few years, I've amassed quite a selection of them. I tried using them in conventional square stitch designs, but the pattern seemed to get lost as the beads turned to fit next to each other. One row showed the flat side of the triangles; the next row showed the tips. This distorted the pattern, but the beads looked like tiles set into grout, which I liked. When I mixed triangle beads of different colors together, I noticed that the back of the beadwork wound up looking entirely different from the front.

After playing around with these unusual effects, I came up with this interesting design for reversible, square stitch bracelets.

These directions are for the two-color bracelet at the top of the page, but you can easily adapt the technique to make the other styles shown. The blue bracelet at left uses beads with slightly rounded edges, which gives the surface a ridged texture that's quite different from the smooth surface you get using sharp-edged triangles. You can use three colors instead of two, mix matte and shiny beads, create stripes or geometric shapes, or work with triangles in other sizes. Just try to choose beads that are uniform in size to minimize distortion at the bracelet's edges.

BRACELET BAND

❶ To determine the finished length of your bracelet, measure your wrist and allow a little extra for ease. Subtract the clasp measurement (including any extra beads used to attach the clasp) to find the length of the beaded band.

❷ Working with a comfortable length of conditioned thread, string a stop bead about 18 in. (45cm) from the thread's tail followed by 11 triangle beads in color A. (This number is given as a suggestion only; make the bracelet as wide as you'd like.)

❸ Work back across the row in square stitch (see "Basics," p. 9), adding one color B bead to each bead in row 1. Make sure to turn the beads so the new row and the previous one are always oriented with a flat edge next to a tip (photo a).

❹ Continue to work in square stitch until you're about eight rows short of the band length determined in step 1.

ADDING A CLASP

Here are a few options for finishing your bracelet:

❶ If you use a slide clasp, work to the full band length determined in step 1, above. Then sew through each of the clasp loops several times before securing the thread (photo b, top). Secure the thread by stitching back and forth through the beads, switching directions a few times, and then trimming the tail close to the beads.

❷ Before attaching a hook or lobster claw clasp, taper the ends as follows: Decrease one stitch on each side for the next four rows or until three beads remain. (The number of decrease rows will vary based on the number of beads in your starting row.) Once you've stitched the last row, bring the thread out on either side of the center bead. Go through the clasp loop and the center bead several times. Secure the thread in the beadwork. Finish the other end by threading the needle on the long

MATERIALS

bracelet at top (p. 65)
- 10g each of two colors of triangle beads, size 10º or 11º
- beading needles, #10 or 12
- Nymo B or Silamide beading thread
- beeswax or Thread Heaven for Nymo
- Fireline fishing line, 6- or 10-lb. test or Power Pro beading thread
- reversible clasp such as S-hook with soldered jump ring, lobster claw, magnetic clasp, or slide clasp

Optional: toggle clasp with 2 4mm round beads, 2 2-3mm round beads, and 2 bead tips

tail left at the beginning of row 1. Taper this end to match and attach the second clasp half (photo b, second to top).

❸ To attach a magnetic clasp, taper the ends and secure the thread tails as in step 2. Anchor a short length of Fireline or Power Pro thread in the beadwork and exit one bead from the edge on the end row. String four beads, half the clasp, and another four beads. Go through the corresponding bead at the other end of the row. Go through the beads and clasp several times to reinforce the loop. Repeat on the other end of the bracelet (photo b, third from top).

❹ For a toggle clasp, taper the ends and secure the thread tails as before. Thread a needle with 12 in. (30cm) of Fireline or Power Pro thread and weave it into the tapered rows as shown in the figure at right. String a 4mm bead, a 2-3mm bead, and a bead tip onto both threads. Pick up an 11º bead on one thread and slide it into the bead tip (photo c). Slide the beads and bead tip close to the beadwork. Knot the threads around the seed bead using a surgeon's knot (see "Basics"). Glue the knot and let it dry, trim the threads, and close the bead tip. Roll the bead tip's hook around the loop on a small toggle clasp (photo b, bottom). Repeat on the other end. – Anne Nikolai-Kloss

a

b

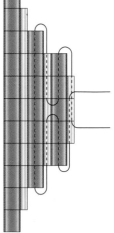

c

Inlaid bead ring

Every so often, I go through all my catalogs looking for new ideas. That's how I noticed a sterling silver channel ring in the Rio Grande catalog. It reminded me of the beautiful cuffs that Amy Karash creates by setting strips of beadwork into channel bracelets. The ring comes in 3mm, 5mm, and 6mm widths, which will accommodate one-, two-, or three-bead-wide strips. I prefer the 6mm ring and like to use Japanese cylinder beads. (Test the beads for color-fastness by applying glue to a few.) I often add an ornament bead, but these rings are less durable than plain ones.

❶ Thread a 1-1½ yd. (.9-1.4m) length of thread on the needle and wax or condition it, if desired.

❷ Square stitch a three-bead-wide strip. String six beads, leaving an 8-10-in. (20-25cm) tail. Go through them again and line them up three over three. String three beads and go through the previous row and the new row **(figure)**. Repeat until the strip is long enough to go around the ring without overlapping or stretching.

❸ (Optional) If adding an ornament bead, sew it onto the middle of the strip and reinforce it with as many thread passes as possible **(photo a)**.

❹ Fit the strip on the channel and weave the ends together firmly, sewing into at least four rows on the starting side **(photo b)**. Thread the needle on the tail and weave through at least four rows on the ending side. Trim both tails.

❺ Hold your ring with the ornament up and apply the glue in an even stream from the ornament base down half the ring. Repeat on the other side of the ornament. Don't get glue on the threads attaching the ornament; it makes them brittle. Apply an even layer of glue to the entire beaded surface of a plain ring.

❻ Suspend the ring on a dowel until it dries completely. – *Kate McKinnon*

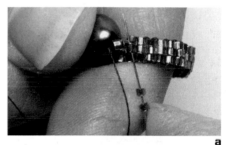

a

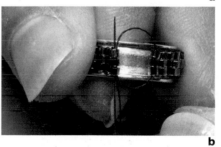

b

MATERIALS

- sterling silver 6mm channel ring (Rio Grande, 800-545-6566)
- 100–150 Japanese cylinder beads
- Nymo B or Silamide beading thread or Fireline fishing line, 6-lb. test
- beading needles, #12 or 13
- cyanoacrylate glue, thin formulation

Optional: ornament bead, beeswax or Thread Heaven for Nymo

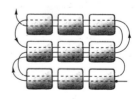

Triangular twist lariat

All beaders have a favorite beading stitch, and square stitch is mine. I find myself returning to it time and time again, especially after a long bout of "free" (and sometimes chaotic) beading. I love that, unlike loomed beadwork, a square stitched piece doesn't have a lot of threads to tie off and hide. Once you're done, you are DONE.

Playing around, I came up with this square stitch variation I call "triangle square stitch." After using it for a variety of necklace styles, I realized it makes a wonderful choker lariat that ties in a loose, open knot. Beaded-fringe tassels made with charms and glass beads finish the ends.

Work triangle square stitch in a pyramidical shape with two-, three-, then four-bead groups. The groups are stitched three to a row and develop into a triangular rope. I like to use a different color for each side to maximize the impact of the lariat. Covering the exposed seams with seed beads in a metallic or contrasting color completes the body of the necklace. Before you tie the lariat, twist it a bit, allowing the different colors to spiral around your neck.

Use round seed beads for the edging because cylinder beads move off the seamline and fray the thread. The edging also receives the most wear so choose non-galvanized beads. All the beads need to have holes big enough to take several passes of thread. You will need to add thread several times in this project. Here is the best method I've found: Make a half-hitch knot (see "Basics," p. 9) against the last bead in a stitch, go back through two beads in the row, knot again, pull the thread

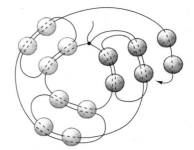

through the rest of the stitch, and clip. These instructions are for a three-color, 33-in. (83cm) lariat. Colors used in the process photos are specified.

❶ On a 3-yd. (2.7m) length of Nymo, string two violet, two opalescent, and two green beads, leaving a tail of at least 18 in. (46cm) for the fringe. Tie the beads into a snug circle with a square knot (see "Basics") and glue the knot.

❷ Pick up two violet beads and sew back through the violet beads on the circle and back again through the beads just added (figure). Pick up two opalescent beads and sew back through the opalescent beads on the first row and back again through the beads just added. Add two green beads in same manner. Add another row of two-bead groups.

❸ Repeat step 2 with three beads in each stitch (photo a). Add three rows of three-bead square stitch.

a

❹ Repeat step 3 with four beads in each group (photo b). Add rows of four-bead square stitch until the lariat is about 32 in. (81cm) long.

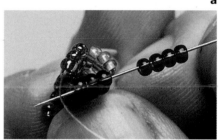

b

❺ To taper the other end, work steps 2 and 3 in reverse, adding three rows of three-bead square stitch, and then three rows of two-bead square stitch. Knot the thread with two half-hitch knots and glue the knot. If possible, leave a tail of 18 in. (46cm) or more on this end for the tassel.

❻ To cover the exposed seams, backstitch a gold seed bead at each row: Knot your thread onto the first row and string a seed bead. Go under the seam thread of the first and second rows. String a bead and go back under the seam thread for the second row, coming up after the third row's seam thread (photo c). Tie a half-hitch knot every four or five beads to secure the edging. Angle your needle in the same direction with each stitch so that the beads are aligned. Add beads in this manner until you complete the seam. Repeat on the other two seams.

c

❼ To make the three-fringe tassel end, thread a needle on the tail and string a large bead to plug the lariat end. String seed beads, decorative beads, and charms to a length of 1-3 in. (2.5-7.6cm). String a "stopper" seed bead,

d

skip it, and sew back up through the fringe (photo d), the plug bead, and one side of the first row of two seed beads. Go back out the plug bead and make another fringe, varying the fringe length. Repeat. Sew up a few rows into the lariat and knot your thread off with two half-hitch knots and glue. At the other end of the lariat, add three fringes in the same manner. – *Pat Chiovarie*

MATERIALS

- size 11º seed beads in three colors, 1 hank or about 20g of each color
- size 11º seed beads, gold or silver, 1 hank or about 20g
- 6–20 decorative beads and charms for fringe
- 2 large round beads (8mm or larger)
- Nymo B or D beading thread in coordinating color
- beading needles, #12
- G-S Hypo Cement or clear nail polish

Brick stitch basics

Blackfeet

Brick stitch, also known as Comanche stitch, is usually started with a single row of beads known as a ladder. Successive rows are added by stringing a bead and then stitching through the loops of thread that run between the beads on the previous row.

LADDER AND BRICK STITCH

1 A ladder of seed or bugle beads is most often used to begin brick stitch: Pick up two beads. Leave a 3-4-in. (9-10cm) tail and go through both beads again in the same direction. Pull the top bead down so the beads are side by side. The

thread exits the bottom of bead #2. String bead #3 and go back through #2 from top to bottom. Come back up #3.

2 String bead #4. Go through #3 from bottom to top and #4 from top to bottom. Add odd-numbered beads like #3 and even-numbered beads like #4.

3 To stabilize the ladder, zigzag back through all the beads.

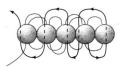

4 Begin each row so no thread shows on the edge: String two beads. Go under the thread between the second and third beads on the ladder from back to front. Pull tight. Go up the

second bead added, then down the first. Come back up the second bead.

5 For the remaining stitches on each row, pick up one bead. Pass the needle under the next loop on the row below

from back to front. Go back up the new bead.

INCREASING BRICK STITCH AT THE END OF A ROW

To increase at the end of a row, work as usual, but instead of going under the loop between the second and third beads, go under the loop between the first and second beads of the row below. Continue in regular brick stitch.

INCREASING BRICK STITCH WITHIN A ROW

To increase within a row, work as usual but attach the increase bead to the same loop that the previous bead is attached to.

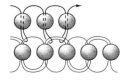

DECREASING BRICK STITCH WITHIN A ROW

To decrease within a row, at the decrease spot, skip over one loop between beads, add a bead, and attach it to the next loop between beads. Pull tight to close up the space.

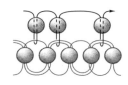

The Blackfeet of northwestern Montana and Canada have a rich tradition of beadwork. The dramatic colors in their beadwork—they often use blues against a deep, rich cranberry red or bright orange and sunny yellow—are exciting and vibrant.

My brick stitch earrings look great in the traditional colors, but they also adapt well to other color schemes, as shown at right. Make your dangles as long or short as you want, but be sure to graduate the lengths symmetrically on both sides. I learned brick stitch from Karen McLaughlin Gallant, who spent a week in Montana in a Native American Ceremonial Arts Camp.

MAKE THE BUGLE BEAD BASE

1 Thread a needle with about 1 yd., (.9m) of conditioned Nymo. Choose seven bugle beads as uniform as possible. (You can make the base ladder longer or shorter, but always use an odd number of beads.) Leaving a 6-8 in. (15-20cm) tail, make a bead ladder with the seven bugle beads (see **figure 1–3** of "Brick stitch basics," at left and **photo a**).

2 Zigzag back through the ladder so your needle is exiting the first bead in the opposite direction of the tail.

MAKE THE SEED BEAD BRICKS

1 String two seed beads and bring the needle under the thread between the second and third bugles on the ladder from back to front (see **figure 4** of "Brick stitch basics" and **photo b**), Go back up the second bead added, down the first, and then back up the second.

2 Add the remaining four stitches on the row by picking up one bead. Go under the next loop on the row below from back to front (**photo c**) and back up the new bead.

3 Repeat steps 1 and 2 four times to make a total of five rows. The last row will have two beads in it.

4 Thread eight beads for the loop that hangs the earring from the finding. (You can make the loop longer or

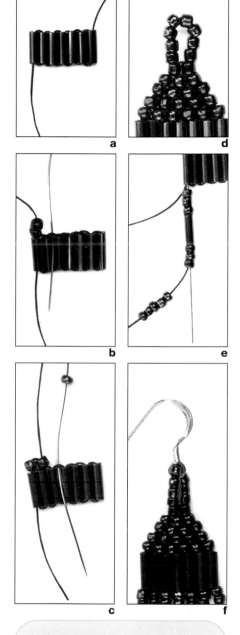

shorter, but always use an even number of beads.) Bring the thread down into the top left seed bead, then back up the top right seed bead and back through the eight loop beads. It's a good idea to reinforce the loop once or twice more **(photo d)**. Sew through the edge beads so your needle exits a bugle bead.

MAKE THE FRINGE DANGLES

❶ With your needle exiting an end bugle, string the fringe beads as desired (here three seeds, a bugle, and eight seeds). Skip five seeds and sew back up through the dangle and end bugle **(photo e)**. The dangle should feel loose and swing easily but be as snug as possible to the bottom of the bugles.

❷ Sew down the second bugle to string the second dangle as you did the first, but string five seeds instead of three at the top,

❸ Make a total of seven graduated dangles as described above.

FINISHING

❶ End the thread by sewing into the top seed bead portion. Go through two or three beads, change direction, and repeat twice. Trim the thread close to the beads.

❷ Open the loop on the earring wire and attach the earring to it **(photo f)**.

❸ Make another earring to match.
– Karen Seaton

MATERIALS

- 14–18 bugle beads (size 3 or 4)
- 3g seed beads (use one size—10º, 11º, or 12º. I prefer 10º, which makes a large, colorful earring.)
- Nymo beading thread, size B or Fireline fishing line 6-lb. test
- beeswax or Thread Heaven for Nymo
- beading needles, #12 or 13
- 2 earring wires with a loop

Brick stitch hearts

In 1990, beading became the culmination of all my earlier artistic endeavors: painting, stained glass, and embroidery. Since then, I've made hundreds of pairs of earrings with brick stitch. These brick stitch heart pins (and earrings) are one of my favorite designs. I usually wear the pin on a lapel or collar, but sometimes I make two—often deleting two beads in row 1—and add earring backs. You can also hang them from earring wires with loops, stitch two together to make a pendant, or attach them to a greeting card, as shown in the inset above.

Begin the heart with the widest row (row 1) worked in ladder stitch. Next, complete the upper lobes of the heart and the lower point in brick stitch. Finally, add fringe dropping it from eight beads along the bottom edge.

❶ Thread a needle with 1½- 2 yd. (1.4-1.8m) of conditioned Nymo. Pick up one light bead (#1) and one dark bead (#2), leaving a 6-in. (15cm) tail to weave in later. Go through both beads. Adjust the beads so they sit side-by-side.

❷ Pick up another dark bead (#3) and go up #2 and back down #3 (see figure 1, "Brick stitch basics," p. 70). Hint: to help keep tension even, pinch the line of woven beads between your left thumb and index finger. Add seven more dark and one more light for a total of ten beads (see figure 2, "Brick stitch basics"). Reinforce this row by zigzagging back through the ladder. End by coming out bead #1 (photo a).

❸ To begin row 2, pick up one light and one dark bead. From back to front, go under the thread between beads #2 and #3 (photo b).

❹ Come back up the dark bead, go down the light bead, and come back up the dark bead (see figure 4, "Brick stitch basics"). Jiggle and tighten the thread to straighten the beads. To complete the row, pick up a dark bead and go under the thread between beads #3 and #4. Come back up this bead (figure 5, "Brick stitch basics"). Repeat to the end of the row 3 then turn the work over to continue.

❺ Repeat steps 3 and 4 to begin row 3 and work across following the chart on page 23.

❻ For row 4, work part way across, adding only three beads—light, dark, light. Row 5 has only two light beads.

❼ Bring the needle down the side through the three light beads on the first lobe and up the adjacent light bead on row 3 (photo c). Repeat step 6 to complete the second lobe.

Sew through the light edge beads and out row 1. Turn the heart over and work eight more rows of brick stitch. The last row has two light beads.

SEA GRASS FRINGE

I got this technique from *Those Bad Bad Beads* by Virginia Blakelock:

❶ Bring your needle out either of the bottom beads. String eight seed beads (the seventh is in the dark heart color). Skipping the last bead, come back through three or four beads **(photo d)**.

❷ String nine more, colored as before, skip the last bead, and come back through five or six beads. Repeat three to five more times. (Adding more beads and going back through different numbers of beads gives the fringe a graduated, more organic look.) Skip the last bead and come back through all the other seed beads in a straight path to the starting bead **(photo e)**.

❸ Come up the starting edge bead and down the next. Make fringes from the bottom eight edge beads. They can be different lengths.

To end a thread, complete a fringe, and then weave diagonally through a few of the heart beads. Make a half-hitch knot (see "Basics," p. 9) between beads. Weave diagonally through a few more beads. Repeat once more before cutting off the end. Begin a new thread the same way, letting it come out a bottom bead to start the next fringe.

COMPLETE THE PROJECT

• To make a pin or post-style earrings: glue the heart to a tie tack back or post-style earring finding and let dry.

• To make hanging earrings: open the loop on an earring wire (see "Basics"), pass it under the thread where the upper lobes meet, and close the loop.

• To make a pendant: make two hearts and stitch them together along the edges. Before closing, stuff lightly with fiberfill. Open a jump ring (see "Basics") and pass one end of it under the thread where the upper lobes meet. Close the jump ring. It is now ready to be used as a pendant for a necklace or lariat.

– Kathleen Burke

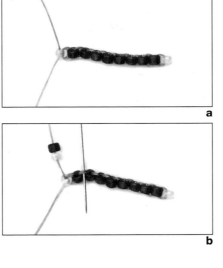

a

b

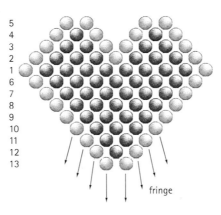

5
4
3
2
1
6
7
8
9
10
11
12
13

fringe

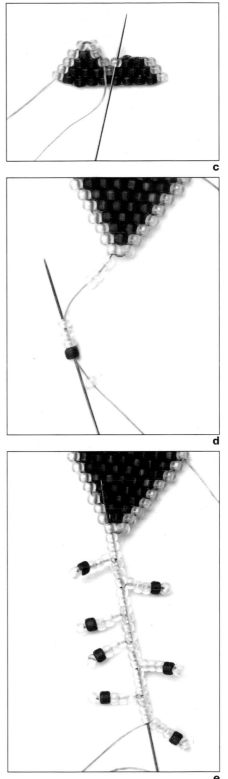

c

d

e

MATERIALS

brick stitch heart

- 5g size 11º Japanese or Japanese cylinder beads, light color
- 5g size 11º Japanese or Japanese cylinder beads, dark color
- Nymo size D or B beading thread
- beading needles, #12

pin or post-style earrings

- tie tack back or 2 post-style earring findings with flat front for gluing
- G-S Hypo Cement or E6000 adhesive

hanging earrings

- 2 earring wires with a loop

Tools: 2 pair of chainnose pliers

pendant

- jump ring
- polyester fiberfill

Tools: 2 pair of chainnose pliers

STITCHING

Hoop dreams

Weave leftover beads into brick stitch curves. Finish with picot edges to score a few three-pointers.

1 Using 2½ ft. (76cm) of thread, tie a half-hitch knot ("Basics," p. 9) on an earring hoop, leaving a 6-in. (15cm) tail. Thread the needle onto the long end.
2 Select a group of size 6º and 8º seed beads. Pick up two beads and slide them against the outer rim of the hoop.

Align the holes so they are parallel to the wire. Take the thread around the hoop, then sew back through the beads as shown in **figure 1**. Pull tight and position the beads against the hoop **(photo a)**.
3 Pick up one bead and go around the hoop. Sew back through the third and second beads, then through the third bead **(figure 2)**. Continue in this modified ladder stitch, picking up a

total of 13 to 15 beads **(photo b)**.
4 Work row 2 in brick stitch (see "Brick stitch basics," p. 70 and **figures 3 and 4**). Pick up two beads, then go around the thread bridge between the second and third beads at the end of row 1. Sew back through the second and first bead added in row 2, then go back through the second bead. Pick up a total of 11 to 14 beads **(photo c)**.
5 For the beads on the outer edge to

fit snugly, you may need to work an increase in brick stitch (see "Brick stitch basics") by connecting two beads to the same thread bridge.

6 For row three, work in brick stitch adding a picot edge as follows: Pick up an 11º and a larger bead.

Skip the 11º and sew back through the new bead as usual. The picot beads sit perpendicular to the other beads on row 3 **(photo d)**.

7 Weave your thread back through the beads, following the thread path. Tie a half-hitch knot between beads, then dab the knot with glue. When the glue dries, weave the tail through the next few beads and cut the excess. Thread your needle on the tail on the other side and repeat.

8 Bend ⅛ in. (3mm) of wire on the hoop earring using your chainnose pliers **(photo e)**.

9 Make a second earring to match the first. – *Carol Cypher*

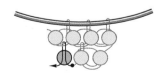

start at knot

figure 1

figure 2

figure 3

figure 4

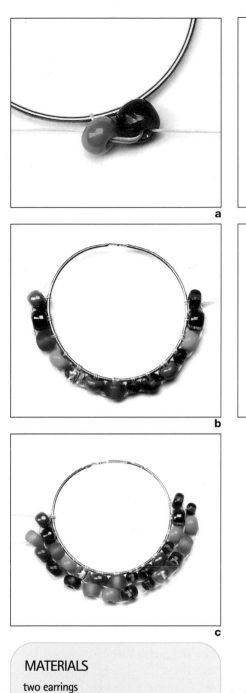

a

b

c

d

e

MATERIALS

two earrings

- 1g assorted seed beads, size 6º to 11º
- 2 25mm wire hoop earrings
- Nymo B or D beading thread
- beeswax
- beading needles, #10 or 12
- G-S Hypo Cement or clear nail polish

Tools: chainnose pliers

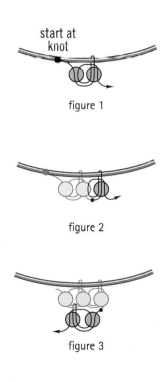

STITCHING

Peyote stitch basics

Peyote stitch, sometimes referred to as "gourd" stitch, is a very popular and versatile weave that is adapted from traditional Native American beadwork. Today, peyote stitch is used in a wide variety of projects, from the basic jewelry styles shown on pages 78-81 to complex, intricate sculptures.

EVEN-COUNT FLAT PEYOTE

1 String one bead and loop through it again in the same direction (remove the extra loop and weave the tail into the work after a few rows). String beads to total an even number. In peyote stitch, rows are nestled together and counted diagonally, so these beads actually comprise the first two rows.

2 To begin row 3 (the numbers in the drawings below indicate rows), pick up a bead and stitch through the second bead from the end. Pick up a bead and go through the fourth bead from the end. Continue in this manner. End by going through the first bead strung.

3 To start row 4 and all other rows, pick up a bead and go through the last bead added on the previous row. To end a thread, weave through the work in a zigzag path, tying two half-hitch knots (see "Basics," p. 9) along the way. Go through a few more beads before trimming the thread close to the work. To resume stitching, anchor a new thread in the work with half-hitch knots, zigzag through the work, and exit the last bead added in the same direction. Continue stitching where you left off.

EVEN-COUNT CIRCULAR PEYOTE

1 String beads to equal the desired circumference. Tie in a circle, leaving some ease.

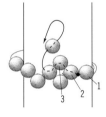

2 Even-numbered beads form row 1 and odd numbered beads, row 2. (Numbers indicate rows.) Put the ring over a form if desired. Go through the first bead to the left of the knot. Pick up a bead (#1 of row 3), skip a bead and go through the next bead. Repeat around until you're back to the start.

3 Since you started with an even number of beads, you need to work a "step up" to be in position for the next row. Go through the first beads on rows 2 and 3. Pick up a bead and go through the second bead of row 3; continue.

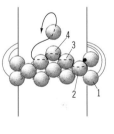

ODD-COUNT CIRCULAR PEYOTE

Start as for circular even-count steps 1-2 above. However, when you begin with an odd number of beads, there won't be a step up; you'll keep spiraling.

PEYOTE STITCH RAPID INCREASE

1 At the point of the increase, pick up two beads instead of one. Pass the needle through the next bead.

2 When you reach the double bead on the next row, go through the first bead, add a bead, and go through the second bead.

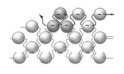

PEYOTE GRADUAL INCREASE

1 The gradual increase takes four rows. At the point of the increase, pick up two thin beads. Go through the next high bead.

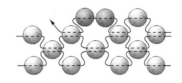

2 When you get to the two thin beads on row 2, go through them as if they were one bead.

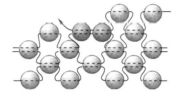

3 On row 3, place two regular-size beads in the two-thin-bead space.

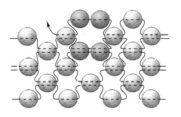

4 When you get to the two beads on the next row, go through the first, pick up a bead, and go through the second.

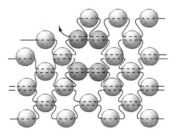

PEYOTE STITCH RAPID DECREASE

1 At the point of the decrease, don't pick up a bead. Instead, go through two beads on the previous row.

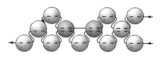

2 When you reach the point where you went through two beads, pick up one bead; continue peyote stitch.

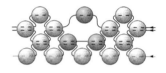

JOIN PEYOTE PIECES

To join two sections of a flat peyote piece invisibly, match up the two pieces so the edge beads fit together. "Zip up" the pieces by zigzagging through each edge bead.

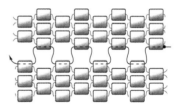

Easy peyote cuff

Using large beads and elastic thread is a good way to learn peyote stitch. The large beads exaggerate the pattern, and the elastic keeps tension even as you stitch.

❶ Thread the needle with a 3-yd. (2.7m) length of elastic. Working with the elastic doubled, string a stop bead (any bead will do) about halfway down the elastic. Take the needle through the bead again to keep it in place, and wrap the long tail of thread around a piece of cardboard so it will stay out of your way (photo a).

❷ String six or eight beads onto the elastic close to the stop bead. These beads comprise the first two rows. Work in even-count flat peyote stitch (see "Peyote stitch basics," p. 76 and photo b at right), stretching the elastic gently to keep the beads in place.

To avoid having a tangled mess of elastic when the working thread is long, hold it away from the beads and keep it under slight tension.

❸ Continue stitching peyote rows until you have about 8 in. (20cm) of thread remaining, and then cut it at the fold, leaving the tails long.

❹ Unwind the elastic on the card. Thread the ends through the needle and continue working in peyote stitch in the opposite direction.

❺ Remove the needle when the thread is about 6 in. (15cm) long and you are in the middle of a row. To add new thread, cut a 4-ft. (1.2m) length of thread and slide the needle to the middle of it. Tie the tails of the new thread to the short tails with a square knot (see "Basics," p. 9) and pull the knot tight. Resume beading with the new thread, pulling the knot and two tails into the first bead. After two to three rows, squeeze a little glue into the bead with the knot. When dry, you can cut off the short tails. Continue in this manner until the length of the bracelet is a comfortable fit around your wrist. End the bracelet with an even number of rows. The thread ends will be on opposite edges.

❻ Stretch the bracelet several times to distribute the thread's tension along its length. Sew the bracelet's ends together by zigzagging between beads (see "Peyote stitch basics" and photo c).

MATERIALS

- 30-40g size 5º hex-cut beads or 4mm square beads (6g of 4mm squares yields 1 in./2.5cm)
- 8-9 yd. (7.3-6.2m) Gossamer Floss or ribbon elastic thread
- tapestry or embroidery needle (size 24) or heavy-duty twisted wire needle
- G-S Hypo Cement

Sew back through several beads in the last row to close the gap on the edge.

❼ Run the tails left in step 3 through several beads in the last row until the two pairs of ends meet. Tighten the elastic so that no thread shows between beads. Tie the ends together with a square knot, pull the knot and two ends into a bead, and squeeze glue into the bead. Trim the ends when dry.

– Mindy Brooks

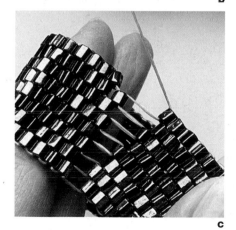

a

b

c

STITCHING

Easy peyote rope

If you want to learn tubular peyote stitch, this is a great project to start with. Created in odd-count peyote with three colors of large beads, it is eye-catching, fashionable, and versatile. Odd-count tubular peyote stitch with large beads is the easiest way to make a peyote rope because the rows have no distinct end. They continue spiraling (see "Peyote stitch basics," p. 76).

String the tube onto a satin cord for an alluringly simple necklace. After you make the first one, try some of the variations that are suggested on page 81 or try some of your own ideas.

PEYOTE STITCH TUBE

❶ Thread a needle with doubled bead cord in a comfortable length. Sew through a contrast-color stop bead twice about 9 in. (23cm) from the tail.

❷ Pick up seven beads in the following order: two color A, two color B, two color C, and one color A. Slide them to the stop bead. Go through the first bead again to close the circle (photo a). Be careful not to split the thread when going back through a bead. When starting a tube, it helps to put it on a chopstick to keep the beadwork tight so you can position new beads correctly.

Keep the new row near the tip of the chopstick. Maintain tension by keeping the cord taut between two fingers of the hand holding the chopstick.

❸ Pick up one A bead, skip the next bead on the circle, and go through the third bead (photo b). Pick up a B bead, skip the next bead on the circle, and go through the fifth bead. Pick up a C bead, skip the next bead on the circle, and go through the next bead, which is the last bead on the first round.

❹ Pick up one A bead and go through the first bead added in round 2 (photo c).

MATERIALS

- size 6º seed beads, 10g in each of three colors
- beading needles or sharps, #8 or 10
- Strength bead cord, size 1-3, or nylon upholstery thread
- 40 in. (1m) 1mm satin cord/rattail
- toggle, lobster claw, or S-hook clasp
- 2 folded crimp ends
- 2 4mm jump rings
- 26-gauge craft wire
- clear nail polish or G-S Hypo Cement

Optional: chopstick

❺ Continue in this fashion, adding one bead per color in each round to form spirals of color **(photo d)**. Don't worry about tension at first. After the third round, give the working thread a gentle tug to snug the beads together. From now on, it will be obvious where each new bead goes, and the tension will take care of itself. When the tube is long enough to hold, you may put the chopstick aside, if you wish.

❻ If you need to add thread, thread a new needle and go through two or three beads two rows back, working toward the old needle. Tie a half-hitch knot (see **photo e** and "Basics," p.9). Follow the old thread path through a few more beads and tie another half-hitch knot. Repeat two more times, ending with the new needle exiting the same bead as the old needle **(photo f)**. Resume work with the new needle. After working a few rows, take the old thread through a few beads and tie a half-hitch knot. Repeat at least twice. End by going through a few beads before cutting off the thread. Dot the knots with glue applied from the tip of the needle.

❼ When you reach the desired length for your necklace, untie the stop bead. Gently pick off the first few rounds of beads until you reach stitches with firm tension. Work the beads you've picked off onto the other end of the tube so the necklace is still the desired length.

❽ To finish, tie a half-hitch knot between the last bead and its neighbor. Go through all the beads at this end of the tube at least once **(photo g)** and knot to the body thread again. Weave back along the thread path as in step 6 to end the thread.

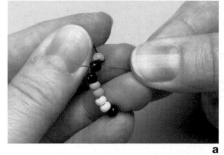

a

b

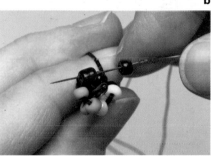

c

d

❾ Repeat step 8 on the other side to end the starting tail.

FINISHING

❶ Use a piece of wire as a harness to string the tube onto satin cord. Cut a piece of craft wire more than twice the length of the tube. Double it and feed the folded end through the tube, being careful not to come through the beadwork. Thread the satin cord through the folded end and pull it back through the tube **(photo h)**. Pull one end of the cord out and center the tube on the cord.

❷ Attach a crimp end to one end of the cord (see "Basics"). Cut the other end of the cord ½-1 in. (1-2.5cm) past

e

f

g

h

the end of the beaded tube. Attach the other crimp end.

❸ Open a jump ring (see "Basics") and slide on one clasp part. Attach the ring to one of the crimp ends and close the ring. Repeat on the other end.

VARIATIONS

- For lengthwise stripes, use different colors on the first row, then match the color to the bead below as you work.
- For horizontal stripes, change colors every few rows.
- For textural variation, use size 5º triangle beads or drop-shaped beads.
  – *Samantha Lynn*

Ndebele herring-bone basics

Ndebele (pronounced en-duh-belly) herringbone is named after the Ndebele tribe in South Africa, with whom this stitch originated. It is characterized by columns of beads that tilt toward each other, creating a texture similar to that of a herringbone fabric.

NDEBELE, FLAT
❶ With 2 yd. (1.8m) of beading cord, stitch a bead ladder (see "Brick stitch basics," p. 70). Zigzag back through the ladder to stabilize it.

❷ To start a row of Ndebele, go up through the first ladder bead. String two beads and go through the second ladder bead (a–b in the figure below). Come back up the third ladder bead and continue until your second row is complete. To turn after adding the last bead of the second row, go down the second-to-last bead of the first row and come back up through the last bead of the second row (c–d). When the working thread is about 6 in. (15cm) long, end it and add a new thread (see "ending and adding thread," at right).

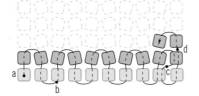

NDEBELE, TUBULAR
To work tubular Ndebele, make a ladder of the desired number of beads (an even number, in this case four) and join it in a ring. String two beads and go down the next bead on the row below (the ladder). Come up the next bead and

repeat. There will be two stitches when you've gone down the fourth bead (a–b in the figure below).

You need to work a "step up" to be in position to start the next row. To do this, come up the bead next to the one your needle is exiting and the first bead of the first stitch (c–d).

Continue adding two beads per stitch and stepping up at the end of each round.

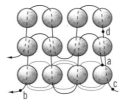

ENDING AND ADDING THREAD
To end, thread the needle on the tail end of the thread (where you cut it from the spool). Insert the needle in the bead where the old thread exits and go down four beads (a–b in the figure below). Go up three beads in the adjacent stack (b–c). Go down two beads in the first stack (c–d). Go up three beads in the second (d–e). Go down four to six beads in the third (e–f). Trim the short tail off and thread the needle on the long end. To add, follow a similar path to the way you ended the old thread, working in the opposite direction.

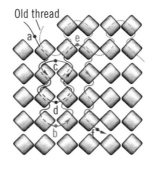

Old thread

Fringed

Contrast matte and shiny seed beads on a flat Ndebele herringbone base. Then embellish the ends with a flower clasp, crystals, and fringe.

BEGIN THE BASE
❶ Start with 3 yd. (2.7m) of thread. Use ladder stitch (as follows) for the base. String two size 8° seed beads. Leave a 10-in. (25cm) tail. Sew back up through the first bead from the tail end. Then go down the second bead (figure 1).
❷ Continue in ladder stitch for a total of four beads (figures 2 and 3).
❸ Zigzag back to the first bead, so the working thread and the tail exit the same bead in opposite directions.
❹ Now switch to Ndebele stitch. String two size 8°s. Go down the second bead and up the third bead in the previous row (figure 4).
❺ String two size 8°s. Go down the fourth bead in the previous row (figure 5).
❻ String one triangle bead to turn the corner. Go up the last bead strung in the previous row (figure 6). Repeat from step 4 until the bracelet fits comfortably around your wrist. Leave the remaining thread to make a loop for the clasp.

CREATE THE CLASP
❶ Weave the 10-in. starting tail up through three rows from the starting edge to exit a bead in one of the two middle columns so the flower or button will be flush with the first row (figure 7, a–b). String one size 11° seed bead, the flower, and an 11°. Go back through the flower and the first 11°. Sew back into the base on the other middle column (fig. 7, b–c). Repeat the thread path to reinforce the flower. Tie off the tail with half-hitch knots (see "Basics," p. 9) and trim.

Ndebele bracelet

❷ For the loop at the other end of the bracelet, bring the needle out the second bead in the last row (**figure 8, a–b**). Make a loop of 11ºs long enough to accommodate the flower clasp (mine is 24 beads long). Go down the third bead in the last row to complete the loop (**fig. 8, b–c**). Go back through the loop again to reinforce it.

❸ Bring the needle through the first two or three seed beads of the loop (fig. 8, c–d).

MAKE THE FRINGE

Alternate straight fringe with branched fringe every few seed beads on the loop.

❶ Straight fringe: Alternate two size 11ºs and a crystal three times. End with three size 11ºs. Skip the last three size 11ºs and go back through all the beads just added (**fig. 8, d–e**). Go through the next few seed beads in the loop.

❷ Branched fringe: String three size 11ºs, an 8º, three size 11ºs, a crystal, and three size 11ºs. Skip the last three size

11ºs and go back through the crystal, and three 11ºs (**fig. 8, e–f**). Add three size 11ºs, a crystal, and three 11ºs. Skip the last three 11ºs and go back through the crystal, three 11ºs, the 8º, and the first three 11ºs (**fig. 8, f–g**). Go through the next few seed beads in the loop.

❸ Continue making fringe around the loop. Tie off the tail and trim.

– Anna Nehs

MATERIALS

- 10g size 8º seed beads
- 6g size 10º triangle beads, for bracelet
- 2g size 11º seed beads, for fringe
- 40 (approx.) 4mm Austrian crystals or fire-polished, faceted beads
- Silamide beading thread or Fireline fishing line 6-lb. test
- beading needles, #12
- flat flower bead for clasp or use a two-hole button

STITCHING

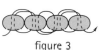

figure 1

figure 2

figure 3

figure 4

figure 5

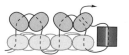

figure 6

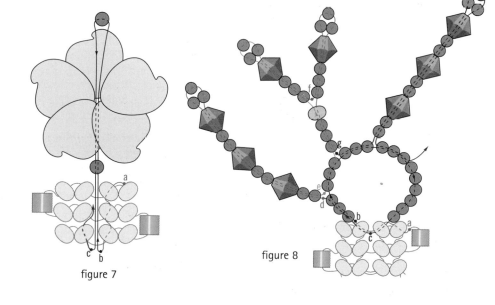

figure 7

figure 8

Endless Ndebele herringbone cuff

Using different shapes and finishes of beads creates a deceptively complicated look in this flat Ndebele herringbone cuff. But it's really easy to stitch and works up quickly.

MAKING THE BASE

❶ Thread a needle with 3 yd. (2.7m) of Fireline. Make a ladder (see "Brick stitch basics," p. 70 and **figures 1–3** at right), alternating a square and a triangle bead twice (four beads). Leave a 6-in. (15cm) tail.

❷ String a square and a triangle. Take the needle down through the second bead and up through the third in the previous row **(figure 4)**.

❸ String a square and a triangle. Take the needle down through the fourth bead (a square) in previous row **(figure 5)**.

❹ String two size 11º seed beads to turn the corner and go up through the last triangle in the new row **(figure 6)**.

❺ Repeat from step 3 until the bracelet fits around the widest part of your hand.

JOINING THE ENDS

❶ Connect the ends by weaving the tail from the end of the bracelet into the first few rows of the beginning of the bracelet. Then weave the tail from the beginning into the last few rows of the end. Make sure the alternating triangle/square pattern matches up.

❷ The square at the edge of the last row will not have two size 11º seed beads next to it yet. Add these beads as you weave the ends together **(figure 7)**. Weave both tails into the work and tie off, using half-hitch knots (see "Basics," p. 9). Trim the tails.

figure 1

figure 2

figure 3

figure 4

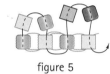

figure 5

figure 6

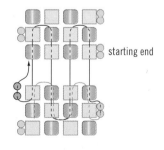

starting end

figure 7

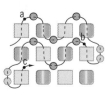

figure 8

STITCHING

FILLING IN THE GAPS

1 Thread a needle with 3 yd. of Fireline and come up through any edge square.

2 Add one size 11º bead and go down through the next triangle in same row.

3 Add one size 11º and go up through the next square in the same row.

4 Add one size 11º bead and go down through the last triangle in the same row. Now pass the needle down the two size 11º beads on the edge and up through the square on the next row below **(figure 8, a–b)**.

5 Repeat from step 2 **(b–c)** until all of the spaces are filled. Weave the thread in and tie off as before. Then trim the tails. – *Anna Nehs*

MATERIALS
- 5-7g 4mm Japanese cube beads
- 5-7g size 5º Japanese triangle beads
- 5-7g size 11º Japanese seed beads
- Fireline fishing line, 6-lb.-test
- beading needles, #10

Tubular herringbone bracelet

Make a sinuous bracelet in a flash as you improve your herringbone skills. Even if you're new to this stitch, you'll find the project quick and enjoyable. Try it with size 5º triangle beads for a chunky feel or streamline it with 8ºs, as shown above. Make different versions and soon you'll be on a bracelet binge—like me.

BRACELET

❶ Measure your wrist and determine the finished length of your bracelet. (Mine is 8 in./20cm.) Subtract the length of your clasp, focal beads, spacers, and 6mm beads. This is the amount of herringbone you'll need for both sides. Divide this number in half to find the length of each side. (Mine are 2 ½ in./6.4cm.)

❷ With 2 yd. (1.8m) of doubled thread, stitch a ladder of four triangle beads in alternating colors **(figure 1)**. Leave a 12-in. (30cm) tail.

❸ Connect bead #4 to bead #1 **(photo a)**. Strengthen by stitching through both beads several times.

❹ Begin a herringbone stitch by holding the beads so the thread exits the top of bead #1. Pick up two triangle beads, keeping like colors stacked together. Go down bead #2 and up bead #3 **(photo b)**.

❺ Add two more beads, alternating the colors as before. Go down bead #4, up bead #1, and through the bead above it **(photo c)**.

❻ Repeat steps 4–5 until you reach your desired length. For 2½ in. (6.4cm) of herringbone, I stitch 23 rows of size 8º seed beads or 17 rows of 5ºs. Note that on the last stitch of each row, you always step up through two beads.

❼ String a spacer, a small focal bead, a spacer, the large focal bead, a spacer, a small focal bead, and a spacer **(figure 2, a–b, and photo d)**.

❽ Pick up two triangle beads. Go back through the focal bead section, then go down the second triangle bead in the last herringbone row **(figure 2, b–c)**.

❾ Work in herringbone as if the focal bead section isn't there. Go up the next triangle bead, through the focal bead section, and pick up two triangle beads **(figure 2, c–d)**.

❿ Go back through the focal bead section, down the last bead, and up the first bead in the row **(figure 2, d–e)**.

⓫ Go through the focal bead section and up a triangle bead.

⓬ Resume picking up pairs of beads and stitching herringbone rows, making the second half of the bracelet to match the first half. Use ladder stitch to connect the last four beads **(figure 1)**.

CLASP

❶ Go down the adjacent triangle bead and up the row's center. Add a spacer, a 6mm bead, six 11º seed beads, half the clasp, and three more 11ºs.

❷ Go back through the first three 11ºs, then tighten to form a loop **(photo e)**.

❸ Go through the 6mm bead, the spacer, and a triangle bead. Go up the row's center then back through the 11ºs to reinforce the loop. Tie three half-hitch knots (see "Basics," p. 9), and dot with glue. When dry, weave in and cut the tail.

❹ At the other end, thread a needle on the tail, and attach the remaining clasp section as before.

– *Dottie Hoeschen*

figure 1

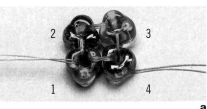

a

b

c

d

e

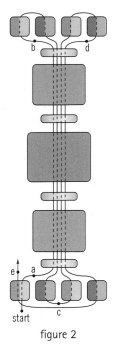

figure 2

MATERIALS

- 134 size 5º or 184 size 8º triangle beads
- 12 size 11º seed beads
- large focal bead
- 2 small focal beads
- 2 6mm beads
- 6 5–6mm spacers
- toggle clasp
- Fireline fishing line, 6-lb. test or Nymo D beading thread conditioned with beeswax
- beading needles, #10 or 12

Right-angle weave basics

Right-angle weave is so named because each bead sits at a right angle to its neighbors. The resulting bead fabric has a lovely drape and texture.

RIGHT-ANGLE WEAVE

❶ To begin, string four beads and tie into a snug circle. Pass the needle through the first three beads again.

❷ Pick up three beads and sew back through the last bead of the previous circle and first new new beads.

❸ Continue adding three beads for each stitch until the first row is the desired length. You are sewing circles in a figure-8 pattern and alternating direction with each stitch.

❹ To begin row 2, sew through the last thee beads of the last stitch on row 1, exiting exiting the top bead of the stitch.

❺ Pick up three beads and sew back through the bead you just exited and the first new bead, sewing in a clockwise direction.

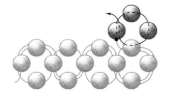

❻ Pick up two beads and sew through the next top bead of the row below and the last bead of the previous stitch. Continue through the two new beads

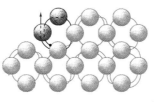

and the next top bead of the row below, sewing counter-clockwise.

❼ Sewing clockwise, pick up two beads, go through the side bead of the previous stitch, the top bead on the row below, and the first new bead. Keep the thread moving in a figure-8. Pick up two beads for the rest of the row.

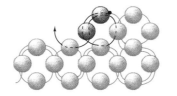

CIRCULAR RIGHT-ANGLE WEAVE

When you are one stitch short of the desired circumference of the first row, exit the end bead of the last stitch, string one bead, go through the first bead of the first stitch, and string one bead. Complete the final stitch of the first row by going back through the end bead of what is now the next-to-last stitch and the first bead added for the final stitch.

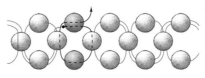

RIGHT-ANGLE WEAVE DECREASE

To decrease, make a normal stitch, but then go through the top beads of the next two stitches on the row below as if they were one stitch.

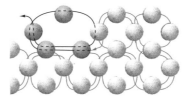

Right-angle weave crystal bracelet

My friend, Cheryl Swanda, owner of My Tyme Beads in Tigard, Oregon, and I were bemoaning the fact that we would probably never own tennis bracelets. She suggested that we make some flashy bracelets out of crystals. It occurred to me that the bicone shape of the crystals might work well in right-angle weave, so I gave it a try.

The crystals took to right-angle weave better than I'd expected. Their bicone backsides meshed with each other perfectly. I stitched until I'd woven the crystals into a panel. It was beautiful but lacked something, so I took out my bead stash and found the perfect spacer bead. As I wove them into the bracelet, it changed before my eyes.

Work the right-angle weave panel in two rows lengthwise. Then embellish it with seed-bead spacers.

❶ With 8 yd. (7.3m) of heavily waxed and doubled thread, string two main-color crystals, half the clasp, and two

a

b

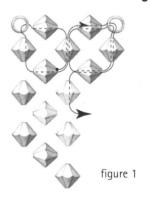

c

more crystals, leaving a 3-in. (7.6cm) tail. Tie the beads into a circle with a square knot (see "Basics," p. 9 and **photo a**). Apply clear nail polish to the knot and let dry.

❷ Work right-angle weave (see "Right-angle weave basics," at left), following the pattern at far right. After adding the eighth set of accent crystals, string two main-color crystals, the clasp, and one main-color crystal. Make sure the bracelet is not twisted and the clasp is oriented correctly.

❸ To start the second row and complete the clasp attachment, string one main color crystal, the second ring on the clasp and two crystals **(figure 1 and photo b)**. Finish the stitch. Continue working in right-angle weave.

❹ For the last stitch, string one crystal, the second ring on the clasp, and one crystal **(photo c)**. Finish the stitch.

❺ Go back through the bracelet, reinforcing with a three-bead zigzag thread path **(figure 2)**, adding a seed bead in the center of each group of four accent beads. Go down one side of the bracelet (red) and up the other (blue).

❻ After reinforcing, start at one corner and add a seed bead between each crystal on the outer edge. If the seed beads overfill the space between crystals, choose a smaller seed bead. Turn at the corner (go through the clasp to reinforce it) and add seed beads down the other side of the bracelet.

– *Judi Mullins*

MATERIALS (7-in./17.8cm bracelet)

- **144** 4mm bicone crystals, main color
- **32** 4mm crystals, accent color
- size 11º or 14º Czech seed beads, accent color
- Nymo B beading thread
- beeswax
- beading needles, size #12 or 13
- 12.5mm two-strand round filigree clasp
- clear nail polish

figure 1

figure 2

Right-angle weave collar

Many years ago I owned a small vintage jewelry and accessory business called Vintage Vogue. When I closed the business, I stashed away much of the jewelry inventory. I just couldn't part with it. It wasn't until recently, when I started the Bloomfield Bead Bunch (BBB), that I remembered my stockpile of old jewelry.

When I got a chance to look through it, I found an intriguing, if dated, necklace to bring to the next BBB meeting. One of the members, Leslee Frumin, studied the dirty, white plastic necklace and, like me, saw potential. She took it home and figured out the pattern—a simple right-angle weave base with a loop fringe. She made a gorgeous rendition in green crystals that inspired all of us to make our own. BBB member Rhonda Gross made the peach and copper version, above. The floral version on p. 91 is by Jackie Scieszka.

a

b

c

d

MATERIALS

dagger fringe necklace
- 300–350 6mm faceted crystals or beads
- 80–100 12-15mm daggers

floral fringe necklace
- 130–150 6mm faceted crystals or beads
- 225–275 8mm glass flower buttons or beads
- 45–55 8 x 10mm glass leaf beads with vertical holes
- 45–55 size 11º seed beads

both necklaces
- 6 size 11º seed beads
- Silamide or Fireline fishing line, 6-lb. test
- 2 bead tips
- clasp
- beading needles, #10 or 12

Tools: chainnose and roundnose pliers

DAGGER FRINGE NECKLACE

❶ Measure your neckline to determine the necklace length. Subtract the length of the clasp.

❷ Cut a length of beading cord ten to twelve times the length determined. String a needle to the middle of the cord and use it doubled. String four 6mm faceted beads 6 in. (15cm) from the tail end. Sew through the first three beads again, drawing all four beads into a tight square.

❸ Using 6mm faceted beads, stitch a chain of four-bead right-angle weave squares (see "Right-angle weave basics," p. 88) the length determined in step 1. Stitch through the last square as if you were preparing to add another square.

❹ String two 11º seed beads, a bead tip, and another seed bead. Sew back through the bead tip and the first two seed beads (photo a). Tighten and sew through the three beads on the square so your needle exits the bottom bead, pointing toward the bead tip.

❺ Pick up two crystals, two daggers, and two crystals. Sew through the bottom crystal on the next square, pointing toward the first square (photo b). Repeat to create an overlapping fringe along the entire chain (photo c).

❻ When you reach the other end, sew through the final square, exiting the top bead and pointing away from the necklace. Repeat step 4. Sew back through the beads, tying three to four half-hitch knots (see "Basics," p. 9) between beads to secure the thread.

Go through a few more beads and trim the thread. Finish the starting thread tails the same way.

❼ Close the bead tips and use roundnose pliers to roll each bead tip's hook around a clasp loop (photo d).

FLOWER FRINGE NECKLACE

The lush version that resembles a Hawaiian lei, at right, is made the same way as the dagger necklace but incorporates more beads in its fringe.

❶ Repeat steps 1-4 above.

❷ String three flower buttons, a leaf bead, and a seed bead. Skip the seed bead, sew up through the leaf bead, and tighten. String three more flower buttons and sew through the bottom crystal on the next square. Repeat to create an overlapping loop fringe along the entire necklace.

❸ Repeat steps 6-7 to complete the necklace. – *Pat Wiley*

STITCHING

Embellished right-angle weave bracelets

Minnesota winters provide ample reason to stay inside, and inspiration often strikes in a snug, toasty house while the wind blows outside. I developed this right-angle weave variation bracelet on just such a winter's day when I was bored with making bracelets using only one row of right-angle weave squares.

To create a more substantial piece, I added another row onto the original eight-bead-square base. Then I pinched the two rows together and joined them. The triangular tube this creates makes an excellent base for all kinds of embellishment. Next, I took the design a step further, adding what I call "wings" of right-angle weave joined to the sides of the triangular tube.

Now I had four surfaces to embellish in any style from fun or casual to tailored, elegant pieces.

Choose round seed beads with smooth edges for this bracelet's right-angle weave structure. Do not use three-cut or hex-cut beads for the structural portion, but cut beads will work well for embellishing because they catch the light and add glitter. The seed beads must also have large holes because you will sew through them at least three times. If a bead seems tight at first, discard it. When your thread gets short, leave it to knot off later and begin a new thread. Don't tie on new threads in the middle of the structural portion. Knots are always weak points, and they can block bead holes that you might need to go through again.

BASIC BRACELET

❶ Thread a needle with 4 ft. (1.2m) of Nymo. String eight beads, leaving a few inches at the end. Tie the beaded thread into a snug circle with a square knot (see "Basics," p. 9). Sew through the first six beads and tighten so that they form a rough square with two beads per side.

❷ Pick up six beads and form the second square by going back through the last two beads you went through in step 1. Sew through the next four of the six beads on the second square (figure 1). Pick up six more beads and sew through the last two beads you went through on the second square.

❸ Continue to add squares until the chain is 6 in. (15cm) long. You will be sewing in a figure-8 pattern with the needle direction reversing on each stitch. Don't be fanatical about pulling the beads tight—they should have a little flexibility. As you add to the bracelet base and embellish it, the stitches will tighten up. After you have completed 6 in., measure it for length around your wrist. The ends should meet without stretching. When you are satisfied with the length, begin the second row.

❹ To begin the second row, sew through the six beads just added for the last square. Pick up six beads and form a square by sewing back through the last two beads you went through on the square below. Continue through the two beads on the next square (figure 2). (Note: This is a deviation from standard right-angle weave, in which stitches are added in figure-8s, not in straight lines.)

❺ Pick up four beads and form the next square by sewing back through the last two beads in the square you just added. Continue through the top two beads of the second square on the first row and through the two beads on the third square of the first row (figure 3). Continue to add squares to complete the second row.

❻ When you reach the end of the second row, your needle should come out between the two rows. Go back through the four beads you just added so that you are between the last and next-to-last squares of the row. Pinch the two rows together so they form a V.

❼ Pick up two beads and sew through the two beads directly across the gap with your needle pointing away from the bracelet (photo a). Pick up two more beads and sew through the two beads opposite and through the next two beads (photo b). Pick up two beads and sew back through the two beads directly across the gap, around through the four beads of the square you have made, and through the next two beads on that row.

❽ Continue adding two-bead stitches between the rows. When you reach the end, make the last connecting stitch between the rows by sewing through the last two beads on the opposite side and completely around the last square.

You have completed the basic bracelet. Begin embellishing or make the winged bracelet following the instructions below.

WINGED BRACELET

❶ To make the wings, you add a row of squares as in steps 4 and 5 above. After completing step 8 above, your needle should come out between the first and second squares of a row.

❷ Pick up six beads and go through the last two beads you went through, continuing through the two beads of the following stitch.

❸ Pick up four beads and form the next square by sewing through the last two beads in the stitch you just added (photo c, p. 94).

❹ Continue through the top two

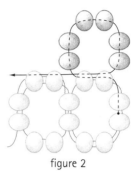

figure 1

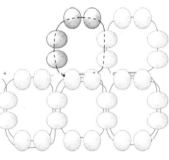

figure 2

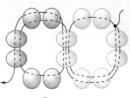

figure 3

a

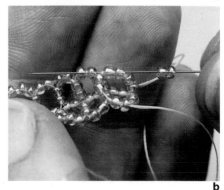

b

beads of the next square on the row and through the two beads on the following square of the row (photo d). Add squares until you reach the end of the row.

❺ Sew through the beads to reach the spot between the first and second stitches on another row. Add the second wing as in steps 2-4.

EMBELLISHMENT

Add embellishments with a diagonal stitch, stringing beads from one corner of each eight-bead square to the opposite corner. I usually string a seed bead, a larger bead or charm, and another seed bead across the stitch. For the winged bracelet, embellish the wings before you embellish the central structure of the bracelet.

❶ Start at the outside corner of

the first square of a row, string your embellishment beads, and sew from the opposite corner through two beads and out to the next square's outer corner (photo e, second wing is hidden underneath). Repeat to the end of the row.

❷ Sew through the beads to the other side of the basic structure or to the other wing and embellish it in the same manner. Angle the stitches on the other side in the opposite direction to create a herringbone pattern. If you don't angle the stitches on the sides in opposite directions, your bracelet will twist. If you make the winged bracelet, keep the embellishment stitches for the wing and the center structure angled the same way on each side to maintain the herringbone pattern. If you don't like this ribbed effect, join the embellishment rows with more beads for a haphazard, casual look.

CLASP

For a sturdy clasp, I recommend running flexible wire through the inside of the triangular structure to eliminate stress on the beadwork.

❶ Cut a piece of flexible wire about 4 in. (10cm) longer than the bracelet. Attach one side of the clasp to the wire with a crimp (see "Basics"). Add a large bead to anchor the clasp to the end of the bracelet. You can bead the wire with coordinating beads or leave it plain.

❷ Thread the wire through the bracelet, using the triangular structure as a tunnel.

❸ Anchor it on the other end with another large bead, and attach the other clasp end with a crimp bead.

❹ Secure the bracelet to the wire at either end by stitching through the structure of the bracelet, the large bead, and the loop that attaches the clasp. Sew back through the large bead and through a few stitches of the bracelet structure. This prevents the bracelet from bunching up on the wire.

❺ Another clasp option is the button and loop clasp used in some of the bracelets on p. 92 and above. If you opt for this type of clasp, anchor the loop and button additions by stitching

through several squares of the bracelet. If you sew through just a few beads at each end, your clasp will break easily.

❻ Complete the bracelet by finishing all the loose threads with half-hitch knots and gluing them. Run the thread tails through a few beads before trimming them. — *Chris Ward*

MATERIALS

- hank size 10º or 11º seed beads, one or more colors
- Nymo D beading thread, in coordinating color
- beading needles, #12
- clear nail polish or G-S Hypo Cement
- beads, crystals, small semi-precious stones or chips, charms, etc. for embellishment, not larger than 3-4mm
- flexible beading wire, .019
- 2 crimp beads
- toggle clasp or large button

Tools: chainnose or crimping pliers and wire cutters

CONTRIBUTORS

Osen Akumasama is a beader based in Seattle, WA.

Mindy Brooks is the editor of *Bead&Button* magazine. Contact her in care of the magazine.

Kathleen Burke teaches beading in her home town, Bisbee, AZ.

Pat Chiovarie teaches beadwork in the Seattle area. Contact her at chiovariestudio@aol.com.

Cathy Collison owns Glass Garden Beads, 413 Division Street South, Northfield, MN 55057; (507) 645-0301, glassgardenbeads.com.

Carol Cypher teaches felting and beading nationwide. Visit her website, carolcypher.com, to see more of her work. Contact her at (845) 384-6417 or chcypher@msn.com.

Lynne Dixon-Speller is a contributing fashion editor for *BeadStyle* magazine. Contact her in care of the magazine.

Joanne Green is a California jewelry designer. Contact her at info@tierracast.com.

Gloria Harris is a retired teacher who now travels and beads.

Dottie Hoeschen teaches beading at My Father's Beads in Coopersberg, PA and bead shows nationwide. Contact her at 3940 Lehnenberg Rd., Riegelsville, PA 18077, stonebrash@juno.com.

Juana Jelen owns Pacific Silverworks. Contact her at 461 E. Main St., Suite 1-A, Ventura, CA 93001, (805) 641-1326, sales@pacificsilverworks.com. Visit her website, pacificsilverworks.com for more information.

Diane Jolie is the managing editor at *Bead&Button* magazine. Contact her in care of the magazine.

Karen Kinney-Drellich is a writer, beader, and quilter from California.

Alice Korach, founding editor of *Bead&Button* magazine, now designs and writes for the *Bead Bugle*. Also a glass artist, her *pâte de verre* creations can be seen on her website, lostwaxglass.com.

Samantha Lynn is a Chicago-based writer, currently trying to sell her first novel and working on a second. She blogs her adventures at livejournal.com/users/robling_t/.

Louise Malcolm is a beader and writer based in Wisconsin.

Kate McKinnon is a prolific bead artist. See her work at katemckinnon.com. Contact her at kate@katemckinnon.com.

Andrea Meloon is a beader from Arizona. Contact her at 12819 W. Georgia Ave., Litchfield Park, AZ 85340, ameloon@cox.net.

Irina Miech owns Eclectica in Brookfield, WI and can be reached at 18900 W. Bluemound Rd., Brookfield, WI 53045-6082, (262) 641-0910, www.eclecticabeads.com.

Judi Mullins teaches beading in Oregon. Contact her at bead.garden@verizon.net.

Anna Nehs is an assistant editor at *Bead&Button*. Contact her in care of the magazine.

Anne Nikolai-Kloss is a contributing editor for *BeadStyle* magazine. Contact her at annekloss@mac.com.

Pam O'Connor is a contributing editor for *Bead&Button* magazine. Contact her at pampal@msn.com.

Cheryl Phelan is an associate editor at *Bead&Button* magazine. Contact her in care of the magazine.

Sue Raasch is a beader from Montana.

Linda Salow can be reached at 270 Big Horn Dr., Estes Park, CO 80517, (970) 577-0439, lsalow@peakpeak.com.

Iris Sandkühler teaches beading in California. Contact her at The Bead Shop 158 University Ave., Palo Alto, CA 94301, (650) 328-5288, elearning@beadshop.com.

Karen Seaton lives in Maryland where she writes, beads, does floral design, and teaches beading to children's groups.

Candace Silber is a Wisconsin beader. Contact her at Candy's Collections, 1508 Jenifer St., Madison, WI 53703, (608) 259-8284.

Nicolette Stessin owns Beadworld in Seattle and can be reached at 9520 Roosevelt Way NE, Seattle, WA 98115, (206) 285-7288.

Beth Stone is a contributing editor for *BeadStyle* magazine. Contact her at (248) 855-9358 or bnshdl@msn.com.

Lisa Olson Tune teaches beading in Oregon. Contact her at Tunebdbdbd@aol.com.

Virginia Tutterow teaches beading classes in Indiana.

Chris Ward is a bead artist from New Mexico. Visit her website, riverspirit.net, to see more of her work. Contact her at 254 San Juan, Los Alamos, NM 87544, artsdesire@comcast.net.

Pat Wiley is a bead artist from Michigan. Contact her at 1780 Alexander Drive, Bloomfield Hills, MI, 48302, (248) 851-5540, wileybead@comcast.net.

Wendy Witchner is a contributing editor for *Bead&Button* and *BeadStyle*. Contact her in care of the magazines.

Sarah K. Young is a Massachusetts beader. Contact her at Beadniks, Vineyard Haven, MA 02568, (508) 627-5693.

Contact *Bead&Button* and *BeadStyle* magazines at PO Box 1612, Waukesha, WI 53187-1612, (262) 796-8776. Visit our websites, www.beadandbutton.com and www.beadstylemag.com to learn more about us.

INDEX